HIKE THE PARKS

ROCKY MOUNTAIN
NATIONAL PARK

HIKE THE PARKS
BEST DAY HIKES, WALKS, AND SIGHTS

ROCKY MOUNTAIN
NATIONAL PARK

BRENDAN LEONARD

MOUNTAINEERS
BOOKS

To Dave Fecik: Thanks for bailing me out of jail that one time so we could do all these hikes together seventeen years later.

MOUNTAINEERS BOOKS is dedicated to the exploration, preservation, and enjoyment of outdoor and wilderness areas.

1001 SW Klickitat Way, Suite 201, Seattle, WA 98134
800-553-4453, www.mountaineersbooks.org

Printed in China

Distributed in the United Kingdom by Cordee, www.cordee.co.uk
First edition, 2021

Copyeditor: Erin Cusick
Design: Jen Grable
Layout: Laura Shaw Design, Inc.
Cartographer: Mike Powers/Honest Maps
All photographs by the author unless credited otherwise
Cover photograph: *Taylor Peak dominates the view from The Loch (Hike 5).*
Back cover photograph: *Longs Peak at sunrise (Hike 25)*
Frontispiece: *Rock formations along the Ute Trail near Poudre Lake (Hike 30)*

Library of Congress Cataloging-in-Publication data is on file for this title at
https://lccn.loc.gov/2020045114 (print) and
https://lccn.loc.gov/2020045115 (ebook)

Mountaineers Books titles may be purchased for corporate, educational, or other promotional sales, and our authors are available for a wide range of events. For information on special discounts or booking an author, contact our customer service at 800-553-4453 or mbooks@mountaineersbooks.org.

Printed on FSC®-certified materials

ISBN (paperback): 978-1-68051-298-4
ISBN (ebook): 978-1-68051-299-1

An independent nonprofit publisher since 1960

CONTENTS

Overview Map.. 7
Hikes at a Glance 9
Visiting Rocky Mountain National Park.......... 13
Planning Your Trip 27
How to Use This Guide 47
Map Legend.. 51

BEAR LAKE ROAD

1 Bear Lake 56
2 Alberta Falls 59
3 Sprague Lake 62
4 Mills Lake 66
5 The Loch 71
6 Odessa Lake via Bear Lake Trailhead.............. 74
7 Four Lakes Loop 78
8 Cub Lake 82
9 Fern Lake 86
10 Bierstadt Lake Loop 90
11 Moraine Park Loop 94
12 Black Lake 99
13 Flattop Mountain and Hallett Peak.................. 104

DEVILS GULCH ROAD

14 Gem Lake... 112
15 Bridal Veil Falls from Cow Creek Trailhead....... 115
16 Black Canyon Trail and Lumpy Ridge Loop 119

COLORADO HIGHWAY 7

17 Lily Lake 128
18 Lily Ridge Trail 131
19 Copeland Falls 133
20 Three Waterfalls................................... 136
21 Lily Mountain....................................... 140
22 Estes Cone via Longs Peak Trailhead 144
23 Twin Sisters Peaks 148
24 Chasm Lake 151
25 Longs Peak via Keyhole Route.................... 155

TRAIL RIDGE ROAD

26 Alpine Ridge Trail.. 164
27 Tundra Communities Trail 167
28 Lake Irene... 170
29 Deer Mountain.. 173
30 Ute Trail from Fall River Pass
   to Milner Pass 177
31 Upper Beaver Meadows Loop.......................... 181
32 Tombstone Ridge via Ute Trail......................... 184

GRAND LAKE ENTRANCE

33 Coyote Valley 192
34 Holzwarth Historic Site..................................... 195
35 Big Meadows from
   Green Mountain Trailhead 198

Contacts 203
Index 205

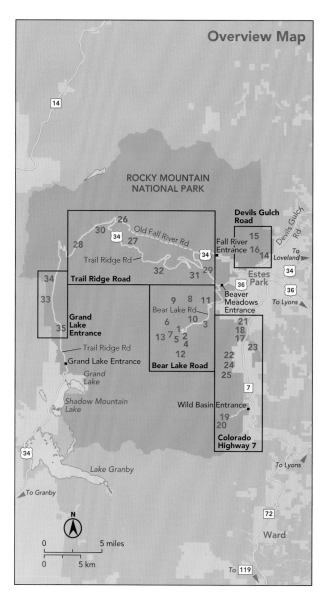

Overview Map

ROCKY MOUNTAIN
NATIONAL PARK

Devils Gulch Road

26
30
28
34
27
Old Fall River Rd
Trail Ridge Rd
32
31
29
Trail Ridge Road
Fall River Entrance
34
15
16
14
Devils Gulch Rd
To Loveland
34
36
To Lyons

34
33
Grand Lake Entrance
35
Trail Ridge Rd
Grand Lake Entrance
Grand Lake

Estes Park
36
Beaver Meadows Entrance

9 8 11
Bear Lake Rd
6 10 3
13 7 5 2
1 4
12
Bear Lake Road

21
18
17
23
22
24
25
7

Shadow Mountain Lake

Wild Basin Entrance
19
20
Colorado Highway 7

34
Lake Granby

To Granby

To Lyons

72
Ward

N

0   5 miles
0   5 km

To 119

HIKES AT A GLANCE

HIKE	DISTANCE miles (km)	ELEVATION GAIN feet (m)	HIGH POINT feet (m)	DIFFICULTY
BEAR LAKE ROAD				
1. Bear Lake	0.8 (1.3)	50 (15)	9490 (2893)	Easy
2. Alberta Falls	1.8 (2.9)	250 (76)	9400 (2865)	Easy
3. Sprague Lake	0.8 (1.3)	Negligible	8690 (2649)	Easy
4. Mills Lake	5.6 (9)	780 (238)	9940 (3030)	Medium
5. The Loch	5.8 (9.3)	1000 (305)	10,180 (3103)	Medium
6. Odessa Lake via Bear Lake Trailhead	8.8 (14.2)	1900 (579)	10,685 (3257)	Medium
7. Four Lakes Loop	5.6 (9)	1030 (314)	10,220 (3115)	Medium
8. Cub Lake	4.8 (7.7)	570 (174)	8670 (2643)	Medium
9. Fern Lake	7.6 (12.2)	1400 (427)	9525 (2903)	Medium
10. Bierstadt Lake Loop	3.2 (5.2)	675 (206)	9455 (2882)	Medium
11. Moraine Park Loop	4.8 (8.5)	100 (31)	8092 (2466)	Medium
12. Black Lake	9.8 (15.8)	1480 (451)	10,640 (3243)	Hard
13. Flattop Mountain and Hallett Peak	10 (16.1)	3250 (991)	12,713 (3875)	Hard

OPPOSITE: *Wildflowers along the Bierstadt Lake Loop (Hike 10)*

HIKE	DISTANCE miles (km)	ELEVATION GAIN feet (m)	HIGH POINT feet (m)	DIFFICULTY
DEVILS GULCH ROAD				
14. Gem Lake	3.5 (5.6)	1000 (305)	8825 (2690)	Medium
15. Bridal Veil Falls from Cow Creek Trailhead	6.2 (10)	990 (302)	8789 (2679)	Medium
16. Black Canyon Trail and Lumpy Ridge Loop	8.2 (13.2)/ 11.2 (18)	1700 (518)/ 2480 (756)	9110 (2777)	Medium/ Hard
COLORADO HIGHWAY 7				
17. Lily Lake	1 (1.6)	Negligible	8935 (2723)	Easy
18. Lily Ridge Trail	1.2 (1.9)	200 (61)	9115 (2778)	Easy
19. Copeland Falls	1 (1.6)	80 (24)	8600 (2621)	Easy
20. Three Waterfalls	5.4 (8.7)	890 (271)	9415 (2870)	Medium
21. Lily Mountain	4 (6.4)	1200 (366)	9786 (2983)	Medium
22. Estes Cone via Longs Peak Trailhead	6.6 (10.6)	1600 (488)	11,006 (3355)	Medium
23. Twin Sisters Peaks	7.2 (11.6)	2350 (716)	11,428 (3483)	Hard
24. Chasm Lake	8.6 (13.8)	2500 (762)	11,800 (3597)	Hard
25. Longs Peak via Keyhole Route	14.8 (23.8)	4855 (1480)	14,259 (4346)	Hard

HIKE	DISTANCE miles (km)	ELEVATION GAIN feet (m)	HIGH POINT feet (m)	DIFFICULTY
TRAIL RIDGE ROAD				
26. Alpine Ridge Trail	0.6 (1)	209 (64)	12,005 (3659)	Easy
27. Tundra Communities Trail	1 (1.6)	175 (53)	12,285 (3745)	Easy
28. Lake Irene	1 (1.6)	100 (31)	10,660 (3249)	Easy
29. Deer Mountain	6.2 (10)	1200 (366)	10,013 (3052)	Medium
30. Ute Trail from Fall River Pass to Milner Pass	4.1 (6.9)	150 (46)	11,764 (3586)	Medium
31. Upper Beaver Meadows Loop	5 (8)	935 (285)	9235 (2815)	Medium
32. Tombstone Ridge via Ute Trail	3.4 (5.5)	1000 (305)	11,655 (3552)	Medium
GRAND LAKE ENTRANCE				
33. Coyote Valley	1 (1.6)	15 (5)	8830 (2691)	Easy
34. Holzwarth Historic Site	1.3 (2.1)	75 (23)	8935 (2723)	Easy
35. Big Meadows from Green Mountain Trailhead	4.8 (7.7)	800 (244)	9475 (2888)	Medium

VISITING ROCKY MOUNTAIN NATIONAL PARK

Dating back almost to its establishment as a national park in 1915, Rocky Mountain National Park has made the alpine accessible to everyone, whether we want to climb a mountain under our own power or not. The park's crown of Continental Divide peaks, rising 6000-plus feet (1829 m) above the gateway town of Estes Park (elevation 7522 feet/2293 m) on its east edge, can be seen up close with just a short drive from town. Trail Ridge Road, completed in 1932, makes it possible for anyone with access to a car to take in a view of the mountains from higher than 12,000 feet (3658 m), see the flora and fauna of the alpine tundra environment, and watch a thunderstorm roll in over the tops of the Rocky Mountains to the west.

For the 82 percent of park visitors who arrive from the east, the mountains of the park mark the beginning of the Rocky Mountains; it's the far eastern edge of the high terrain that runs across the Lower 48 from Mexico to Canada, where the plains rise up thousands of feet into majestic peaks. The park is home to megafauna, like elk, moose, and black bears, as well as animals unique to alpine environments, including yellow-bellied marmot and bighorn sheep. Park visitors have a chance to take in the high-altitude scenery

OPPOSITE: *If you time it right, the east face of Longs Peak lit up at sunrise will be your reward in the final mile of the trail leading to Chasm Lake (Hike 24).*

and wildlife without stepping more than a half mile from a car, and can also walk for days into the mountain wilderness, miles from the nearest road. Elk on the east side of the park, accustomed to humans and cars, can be seen grazing on the fairways of the Estes Park Golf Course, while elk high on the west side of the park seem wary of the rare human hiking through alpine tundra.

This book celebrates the accessibility of the park's mountains by curating a variety of hikes, from stroller-friendly walks around lakes to high-altitude peak-bagging adventures, all within a short drive of a post-hike pizza, beer, or ice cream cone back in civilization afterward—or a seat in a camp chair in front of a fire in one of the park's campgrounds.

HUMAN HISTORY

The human history of the area we've called Rocky Mountain National Park for the past hundred years goes back to the time the glaciers that had covered the area receded, roughly eleven thousand years ago. Using the route that is now Trail Ridge Road, early humans hunted mammoth and, later, bison. Sometime between AD 1000 and 1300, Ute people moved into the area, although never permanently, and dominated until the early 1800s, when they were pushed out by the Arapaho people. The Ute and Arapaho people used the Ute Trail to move to and from the Great Plains, where they hunted bison. The Arapaho left the area prior to the 1860s, when white settlers began to arrive.

In 1803, the United States government claimed the land through the Louisiana Purchase, and the 1800s brought the first exploration by non-indigenous peoples, including hopeful miners, homesteaders, and hunters, and with them, tourists. Around the turn of the twentieth century, the movement

OPPOSITE: *A hiker passes through a stand of aspens on the trail to Bridal Veil Falls (Hike 15).*

A marker along the Tundra Communities Trail (Hike 27) displays the distance to other national parks.

to preserve wild lands in the United States gained momentum, and by 1909, local guide and lodge owner Enos Mills began a campaign of lecturing, letter writing, and lobbying to establish a national park in the area—what would be the tenth US national park. The efforts of Mills and other advocates paid off in 1915, when President Woodrow Wilson signed the Rocky Mountain National Park Act, officially protecting the park, then 358 square miles (927 square km). Through acquisitions and donations since the park's creation, it has since grown to the 415 square miles (1075 square km) it covers today.

ARAPAHO NAMES

In 1914, the Colorado Mountain Club arranged for Arapaho elders living on the Wind River Reservation to take a two-week pack trip through what is now Rocky Mountain National Park, in order to provide the Arapaho names for landmarks in the area. Oliver Toll, who became the trip's "accidental ethnographer," recorded place names like the Ute Trail, Niwot Ridge, Lumpy Ridge, and the Never Summer Mountains, which are still used today (even though some people question the translations).

FLORA AND FAUNA

The land of Rocky Mountain National Park spans three classifications of ecosystems, home to a diverse collection of plant and animal life: montane (elevations up to 9500 feet/2896 m), subalpine (elevations between 9000 feet/2743 m and 11,000 feet/3353 m), and alpine tundra (elevations higher than 11,000 feet/3353 m). From the more temperate valley floors to the harsh conditions of the alpine tundra, it's all connected. Here are a few selected animals and plants you might see on a visit to the park:

ELK

Elk are arguably the most famous animals in the park, roaming from the high-altitude alpine tundra all the way down to the golf courses in Estes Park. Elk travel in herds that can number in the hundreds. Fall is their mating season, and if you're anywhere in the vicinity of a herd at that time of year,

you might hear the bugling of bull elk. Only male elk have antlers, which they grow in the spring and shed in the winter. If you're wondering how close you should get to an elk, consider this: Elk can run 45 miles per hour (72 kmph). Stay at least 75 feet away (23 m).

BIGHORN SHEEP

The bighorn sheep, Colorado's official state animal, is also the symbol of Rocky Mountain National Park. It's estimated that more than six hundred bighorn sheep live in the park, eating grasses and other vegetation and using their grippy hooves and soles to avoid predators by traversing cliffs and ledges. Their horns are permanent and can weigh up to thirty pounds (13.6 kg), and they use them to head-butt each other at speeds of up to 40 miles per hour (64 kmph) in mating rituals. In late spring and early summer, bighorn sheep are known to travel down from the Mummy Range to Sheep Lakes in the middle of the day to get nutrients from the plants and soil.

BEARS

Sightings of black bears—whose fur, contrary to their name, can be brown—are uncommon in Rocky Mountain National Park, but enough black bears call the park home for bear canisters to be required for backcountry travel, and for bear-proof food lockers to be provided in park campgrounds. Black bears weigh between 200 and 600 pounds, can run 25 to 30 mph, and generally avoid humans.

MARMOTS

Cousins of the more famous groundhog, marmots are the huskiest members of the squirrel family, inhabiting rocky

OPPOSITE: *Wildflowers along the Black Canyon Trail (Hike 16)*

areas in the harsh alpine environment and digging labyrinthine tunnel systems underneath boulders, where they live in groups of ten to twenty. They hibernate for more than half the year, bedding down for the winter in late September or early October and staying in until April or May. If you hear a marmot whistle in the alpine, it is likely signaling to other marmots that a potential danger is nearby (you) so they can take cover in tunnels.

FISH

Several species of fish can be found in the lakes, rivers, and streams in Rocky Mountain National Park, and six species are known to be native to the park: western longnose sucker, western white sucker, mottled sculpin, cutthroat trout, Colorado River cutthroat trout, and the greenback cutthroat trout, which is the official Colorado state fish and is currently classified as threatened on the endangered species list. All greenback cutthroat trout in Rocky Mountain National Park are catch-and-release.

WILDFLOWERS

From late spring to late summer, wildflower blooms bring a palette of red, purple, white, and yellow to trail sides and meadows all over the park. Some of the flowers more commonly seen on the hikes in this book are cow parsnips, arnica, alpine avens, scarlet paintbrush, fireweed, Bigelow's tansyaster, and lupine. The Colorado state flower, the purple-and-white Colorado columbine, is also found in the park.

TREES

Rocky Mountain National Park's mountainsides are thick with evergreen trees, including Douglas fir, lodgepole pine, ponderosa pine, Colorado blue spruce, and Engelmann spruce, and in the rocky and windiest areas of the park, gnarly limber pines can be found, their trunks and limbs twisted dramatically by wind. Stands of aspen can also be found throughout the park, bringing fall color to the mountains when their leaves turn golden in autumn.

ALPINE TUNDRA PLANTS

Above 11,500 feet (3505 m), you won't see tall trees, but the ground at that altitude is far from barren. Many hardy shrubs, grasses, and lichen thrive in the short growing season and harsh environment of the alpine tundra. Low-growing, wind-twisted fir and spruce trees can be several hundred to a thousand years old. These trees, called *Krummholz* (a German word meaning "wood that is crooked, twisted, or bent") mark the upper limit of tree growth and the transition to alpine tundra, where a number of low-to-the-ground grasses and sedges carpet the mountain slopes.

KEY STATISTICS

- Established: January 26, 1915
- Acreage: 265,807 acres (107,568 hectares); includes inholdings
- Square miles: 415 square miles (1075 square km)
- Designated as wilderness: 94.9 percent (252,298 acres/ 102,101 hectares)
- Tundra acres: 89,099 acres (36,057 hectares)
- Named peaks: 124 named peaks 8789 feet (2679 m) or higher; 118 above 10,000 feet (3048 m), 98 above 11,000 feet (3353 m), 77 above 12,000 feet (3658 m), 20 above 13,000 feet (3692 m), 1 above 14,000 feet (4267 m)
- High point: Longs Peak at 14,259 feet (4346 m)
- Lakes: 147
- Average annual visitation: 4.5 million
- Hiking trails: Approximately 355 miles (571 km)

MUST-SEE SIGHTS AND ACTIVITIES

This list primarily includes activities other than hiking, but there are two short (1-mile) hikes that are family-friendly. The others provide easy, accessible diversions and sightseeing opportunities unique to Rocky Mountain National Park.

TRAIL RIDGE ROAD

Trail Ridge Road, the park's paved "highway to the sky," climbs more than 4000 feet (1219 m) from either side of the park to its high point at 12,183 feet (3713 m), passing through a variety of mountain environments on its way to the alpine tundra. It's a winding, adventurous drive with multiple pull-offs and viewpoints along its 48-mile length from Estes Park to Grand Lake. It can be taken as quickly or as slowly as you'd like, treated as simply a scenic drive (allow 2 to 4 hours, depending on traffic), or an all-day sightseeing tour by stopping at all the points of interest along the way.

ALPINE VISITOR CENTER

The Alpine Visitor Center, at Fall River Pass at 11,796 feet (3595 m), is the highest visitor center in the National Park system, and is the turnaround point for many visitors who have driven up Trail Ridge Road from either side of the park. It has educational displays about the tundra environment, wildlife and plant life, and human history, as well as mountain views inside and out. Rangers are available to answer questions, and a small gift shop sells maps, books, and some souvenirs (the Trail Ridge Store, next door to the Alpine Visitor Center, has a larger gift shop and a café).

SHEEP LAKES

It's certainly not guaranteed that you'll see a bighorn sheep on your visit to Rocky Mountain National Park, but your best

OPPOSITE: *The view out the door of the Agnes Vaille Shelter on Longs Peak (Hike 25)*

Helpful signage on the Fern Lake Trail (Hike 9)

shot is visiting Sheep Lakes (not just a clever nickname) in Horseshoe Park, 1.8 miles (2.9 km) west of the Fall River Entrance Station on US Highway 34. Generally, if groups of sheep are in the area, they'll appear near Sheep Lakes between 9:00 AM and 3:00 PM as they make their way down from the Mummy Range to graze and then head back when they're done. As always with wildlife, stay at least 75 feet (23 m) from sheep.

FOREST CANYON OVERLOOK

There are many places in the park that provide views of mountains, but the Forest Canyon Overlook is one of the more dramatic views. A few steps off Trail Ridge Road, the viewpoint looks from the tops of the peaks across the canyon all the way down into Forest Canyon, 3000-plus feet (914 m) of relief, not to mention the panorama of peaks all the way to 14,259-foot (4346 m) Longs Peak to the east. The Forest

Canyon Overlook is on the west side of Trail Ridge Road, 10.9 miles (17.6 km) west of Deer Ridge Junction.

OLD FALL RIVER ROAD

Before the completion of Trail Ridge Road in 1932, Fall River Road carried visitors into the park's interior up to Fall River Pass (11,796 feet/3595 m), linking Estes Park on the east side to Grand Lake on the west side. The one-way road is still open seasonally, but the sparser traffic, tight turns, lack of guardrails, and dirt surface (only the first third of the road is paved) give it an adventurous, backcountry feel. Old Fall River Road begins 2.1 miles (3.4 km) west of the Fall River Entrance Station on US 34, and heads west 11 miles to the Alpine Visitor Center. The speed limit on the road is 15 miles per hour (24 kmph), so expect to take at least an hour for the drive, even if you don't stop to get out and take photos.

BEAR LAKE INTERPRETIVE HIKE

The hike around Bear Lake (Hike 1) is one of the most popular hikes in the park because of its ease of access, friendly grade, and short length. To learn more about the area, stop at the NPS booth at the Bear Lake Trailhead and pick up the Rocky Mountain Conservancy guide booklet to the trail (for a small fee)—it details the plants, animals, geology, and human history of Bear Lake, through thirty marked stops along the path.

TUNDRA COMMUNITIES TRAIL

Just over 15 miles from the Beaver Meadows Entrance Station, the 1-mile Tundra Communities Trail (Hike 27) enables close-up access to the plants and wildlife of the alpine tundra in the thin air and harsh climate above 12,000 feet (3658 m), as well as expansive views of the roof of Rocky Mountain National Park and other peaks along the Continental Divide. A short, kid-friendly rock scramble leads up to the best viewpoint here.

PLANNING YOUR TRIP

This section covers the resources and information you need to plan a trip to Rocky Mountain National Park, including suggested itineraries, locations of visitor centers, weather, campground details, fees and permits, and park rules and regulations.

GETTING TO THE PARK

During the busy season, the park recommends using the shuttle system (open May 23 to October 18) to access busy trailheads on the east side of the park, where several parking lots fill quickly and early in the morning. The shuttle will get you to trailheads for many of the most popular hikes, including Bear Lake, Glacier Gorge, Cub Lake, Fern Lake, Sprague Lake, and Bierstadt Lake.

During summer and fall weekends, when the lot for the park's shuttle also fills up quickly, minimize frustration by parking at the Estes Park Visitor Center and then taking the Hiker Shuttle Express bus to the Park & Ride lot; from there you can take the Park & Ride shuttle to your trailhead.

Shuttle schedules vary with more runs during the heart of the day and fewer in the early morning or evening hours. Most park-operated shuttles are wheelchair accessible. Fully-trained service animals are allowed on shuttles, but pets are not. There is no park-run shuttle service on the west side of the park.

OPPOSITE: *A hiker on the trail climbing up to Bierstadt Lake (Hike 10), with the peaks of the Continental Divide off in the distance*

SUGGESTED ITINERARIES

These itineraries are designed to pack a wide variety of experiences into either a one- or three-day visit.

ONE DAY

Hopefully you've got more than one day to explore Rocky Mountain National Park, but if you don't (or you just want some suggestions), here's an ambitious-but-doable itinerary that provides a tour of a couple of the best spots in the park.

- Watch the sunrise at Sprague Lake.
- Hike the Four Lakes Loop (Hike 7) or the Bear Lake Trail (Hike 1).
- Drive Trail Ridge Road to the Forest Canyon Overlook and then the Alpine Visitor Center.
- Hike the Tundra Communities Trail (Hike 27), weather permitting. Be aware that this trail is fairly exposed—not ideal if the forecast calls for an afternoon thunderstorm.

THREE DAYS

This three-day itinerary combines a selection of diverse hikes with some mellow sightseeing drives and walks, and spans the park from east to west.

Day One:
- Hike to Mills Lake (Hike 4) or do the Four Lakes Loop (Hike 7) in the morning.
- Drive down to Sheep Lakes by early afternoon for a chance to see grazing bighorn sheep.

Day Two:
- Watch the sunrise at Sprague Lake.
- Hike up Deer Mountain (Hike 29) or Lily Mountain (Hike 21).
- Hike the Moraine Park Loop (Hike 11) in the afternoon.

A section of trail on the Upper Beaver Meadows Loop (Hike 31)

Day Three:

- Drive Old Fall River Road to Fall River Pass and the Alpine Visitor Center.
- Hike the Alpine Ridge Trail (Hike 26).
- Drive Trail Ridge Road down to the east, stopping to hike the Tundra Communities Trail (Hike 27) and take photos at the Forest Canyon Overlook.

VISITOR CENTERS

The **Alpine Visitor Center** is located on Fall River Pass (11,796 feet/3595 m) at the junction of Trail Ridge and Old Fall River Roads, and is open Memorial Day through mid-October, depending on weather. Hours vary by season. See Contacts for details for each of the centers.

The **Beaver Meadows Visitor Center** is located just inside the park's main entrance on the east side of the park at 1000 US Highway 36.

The **Fall River Visitor Center** is located on the east side of the park at 3450 Fall River Road, five miles west of Estes Park.

The **Kawuneeche Visitor Center** is located at the park's west entrance at 16018 US Highway 34.

GATEWAY TO THE PARK

Estes Park is best known as the gateway to Rocky Mountain National Park, for good reason: The majority of visitors to the park enter from the east side, and the most popular park entrances are accessed from Estes Park. The town sits at an elevation of 7522 feet (2292 m), and from many spots in town, you can see the high peaks of Rocky Mountain National Park, as well as park features like the granite formations of Lumpy Ridge. Estes Park offers all the amenities you might need: hotels and vacation rentals, gas, restaurants, grocery stores, outdoor gear shops, and equipment rental.

The Estes Park Visitor Center (see Contacts), located at 500 Big Thompson Avenue in Estes Park, provides information on the town, the park, and the surrounding area. Between May 23 and October 18, the Estes Hiker Shuttle Express bus travels between the Estes Park Visitor Center and the Park & Ride lot inside the park where you can access shuttle buses to its popular trailheads. The Hiker Shuttle Express bus operates from 7:30 AM to 8:00 PM.

OPPOSITE: *A view of Hallett Peak from the Flattop Mountain Trail (Hike 13)*

WEATHER

One piece of advice for exploring Rocky Mountain National Park at any time of year: bring more clothes than you think you need, including a rain jacket. The weather in the park can change quickly, and even when it's sunny and warm in Estes Park, it can be cold, windy, and snowing up on Trail Ridge Road (yes, even in summer). Afternoon thunderstorms are common (almost daily) in the summer, and almost every hike in this book has a note of warning about exposure to thunderstorms. Lightning is a very real danger in the mountains, so check weather forecasts, plan accordingly, and watch for clouds building into storms in the early afternoon. Summer hiking, even at 10,000 feet (3048 m), can be warm in full sun but also exposed to a chilling mountain wind at the next turn. Packing a few light layers, a hat, and a rain jacket can make the difference between having a comfortable day out and suffering near-hypothermia.

WHEN TO VISIT

Rocky Mountain National Park is open 24 hours a day, 365 days a year, but many roads and facilities—such as Trail Ridge Road, which is open from approximately mid-May through mid-October, depending on weather—are open only during the summer season. The majority of the park's hiking trails are snow-free from early June through late September, and campgrounds in the park typically open for the summer around the last week of May and stay open through mid-September (and some through mid-October). Summer brings the mildest temperatures to the park, but as elevations vary widely, temperatures can drop below freezing and, it bears repeating, snowstorms can happen in nearly any month, even summer.

CAMPGROUNDS

Rocky Mountain National Park has five campgrounds, three of which are reservable, and two of which are first come, first served. Reservations can be made up to six months in advance of your visit, and the park strongly recommends making advance reservations when possible, as spots in campgrounds are filled every night by reservation. Outside of the park on both the east and west sides, several public campgrounds and several Forest Service campgrounds are available.

With the exception of Longs Peak and Moraine Park Campgrounds, the campgrounds in the park open for the summer season typically sometime in late May and close sometime in mid-September to mid-October each year. Longs Peak Campground has a shorter season, typically opening in late June and closing in early September, while Moraine Park is open year-round, with sixty-four of its sites available during the off-season on a first-come, first-served basis. For details on opening and closing dates, and to make reservations, visit the Campgrounds page on the Rocky Mountain National Park website (see Contacts).

Llamas pack in gear to Calypso Cascades and Ouzel Falls (Hike 20).

ASPENGLEN CAMPGROUND

The Aspenglen Campground, just inside the east side of the park at the Fall River Entrance on US Highway 34, has fifty-two campsites (all reservable), trash and recycling receptacles, food storage lockers, staff on site, an amphitheater, flush toilets, drinking water available seasonally, and ice and firewood for sale seasonally. There is no cell phone reception.

GLACIER BASIN CAMPGROUND

The Glacier Basin Campground, 5.8 miles (9.3 km) west on Bear Lake Road from the Beaver Meadows Entrance on the east side of the park, has 150 campsites (all reservable), trash and recycling receptacles, food storage lockers, staff on site, an amphitheater, flush toilets, drinking water and an

RV dump station available seasonally, and ice and firewood for sale seasonally. There is no cell phone reception.

MORAINE PARK CAMPGROUND

The Moraine Park Campground on US 36, 2.2 miles from the Beaver Meadows Entrance on the east side of the park, has 244 campsites (239 of which are reservable during the season), trash and recycling receptacles, food storage lockers, staff on site, an amphitheater, drinking water and an RV dump station available seasonally, and ice and firewood for sale seasonally. Flush toilets are available seasonally, and vault toilets are available year-round. There is no cell phone reception.

LONGS PEAK CAMPGROUND

The Longs Peak Campground, located just north of the Longs Peak Trailhead, 9 miles south of Estes Park on Colorado Highway 7, is first come, first served, and has 26 tent-only sites. It has trash and recycling receptacles, food storage lockers, drinking water available seasonally, and vault toilets. There is no cell phone reception.

TIMBER CREEK CAMPGROUND

The Timber Creek Campground, the only park service campground on the west side of the park, is located 8 miles north of the Grand Lake Entrance Station on US 34. It has 98 campsites, all first come, first served. Because of a pine beetle infestation, almost all the trees at the Timber Creek Campground had to be removed, so there is no shade at campsites. It has trash and recycling receptacles, staff on site, an amphitheater, flush toilets, drinking water and an RV dump station available seasonally, and firewood for sale seasonally. There is no cell phone reception.

PARK RULES AND REGULATIONS

Rocky Mountain National Park is the third most visited national park in the United States. Such popularity calls for everyone to follow some commonsense regulations.

FEES

Entry to Rocky Mountain National Park requires paying fees when entering the east side of the park at the Beaver Meadows Entrance on US 36, the Fall River Entrance on US 34, and the Wild Basin Entrance off of CO 7, and on the west side of the park at the Grand Lake Entrance on US 34. Hikes using the Cow Creek Trailhead, Lumpy Ridge Trailhead, Longs Peak Trailhead, Lily Lake Trailhead, and Twin Sisters Trailhead do not require paying entrance fees. See the Fees & Passes page on the park's website for details.

A sign at the top of the Keyhole Route (Hike 25) on the summit of Longs Peak

DOGS

As wonderful as it can be to have your best four-legged friend along with you, dogs are prohibited on all the routes within this guide. As with most national parks, dogs are allowed on paved and unpaved roads in Rocky Mountain National Park so long as they are leashed, and they are also welcome within campgrounds and picnic areas. If you find this restriction onerous, bear in mind that the park has deemed that pets pose a threat and disruption to wildlife and, given the park's mandate to protect the flora and fauna within it, wildlife gets priority. It is prohibited to leave a pet unattended and tied to an object.

FISHING

With the exception of Bear Lake, where it is prohibited, fishing is allowed throughout Rocky Mountain National Park, but requires a Colorado fishing license for anyone sixteen years or older. In addition, those twelve years old or younger may use bait in waters open to fishing, except in designated catch-and-release areas. For a list of lakes that are known to have fish, as well as details of fishing regulations, visit www.nps .gov/romo/planyourvisit/fishing.htm.

THE FIRST ENTRANCE FEE

The first person to pay an entrance fee to Rocky Mountain National Park was Abner Sprague, in 1939. Sprague homesteaded in the Moraine Park and built Sprague's Ranch near the present-day parking lot of Sprague Lake (named after Sprague), with his wife, Alberta, for whom Alberta Falls is named.

OPPOSITE: *You pass through dense forest on the trail up to the Twin Sisters Peaks summits (Hike 23).*

BACKCOUNTRY CAMPING

Large parts of the park are open to public use, specifically backcountry camping, outside of daylight hours. Camping in the park is subject to a fee and is restricted to designated campgrounds or in the backcountry with an overnight wilderness permit. Permits are available at park Wilderness Permit and Information Offices—the Wilderness Office on the east side of the park is adjacent to the Beaver Meadows Visitor Center, and on the west side of the park, the Wilderness Office is located inside the Kawuneeche Visitor Center.

Campfires are allowed only in certain areas where metal fire rings are provided.

When backcountry camping below tree line or in the Boulderfield of Longs Peak between April 1 and October 31, the park requires that all food items and garbage be secured inside a hard-sided commercially made carry-in/carry-out bear-resistant food storage container.

Always select a durable surface to camp on, and pack out everything that you bring in, including used toilet paper; toilet paper takes some time to decompose in the alpine environment and may even be dug up by animals, ruining another hiker's experience. As for solid human waste, always bury it in cat holes at least 6 to 8 inches (15 to 20 cm) deep. For more information on backpacking and backcountry permits, visit www.nps.gov/romo/planyourvisit/wilderness-camping.htm.

FIREARMS

Federal law allows people who can legally possess firearms to carry them within the park provided they comply with state laws and regulations. Firearms are not permitted in certain facilities, and those facilities are always marked.

DRONES

Drones are remote-operated, unmanned aircraft that people often use for videography or for fun. However, to limit noise pollution, protect habitats, protect wildlife, and preserve scenic and wilderness values, the park forbids the use of drones. The only exception is if you have written permission from the park's superintendent.

WILDLIFE

The park has a large population of free-roaming wild animals, some of which are unpredictable and potentially dangerous. Wildlife viewing is encouraged but only from a safe distance. Approaching within 75 feet (23 m) of any wild animal, including nesting birds, or within any distance that disturbs or interferes with their free movement or natural behavior, is prohibited.

CAMPFIRES

Campfires are permitted only within designated campfire rings. Do your part to avoid starting more forest fires that destroy habitat and scar the landscape.

LEAVE NO TRACE PRINCIPLES

In any place this popular, it is imperative that hikers adhere to Leave No Trace (LNT) principles. Although LNT principles don't always have the weight of the law behind them, it's critical to follow these guidelines because your caution and care help mitigate overuse. It also ensures that everybody else can enjoy the park as much as you do. You may have noticed that some of these have already been mentioned in the park rules and regulations, but when it comes to hiking responsibly, these principles can't be stressed enough.

PLAN AHEAD AND PREPARE

Nothing guarantees success in life as much as preparation, and that same rule carries through to hiking. Many hikers get into trouble because they run into conditions they did not prepare for; a lot of difficulties hikers encounter are wholly avoidable. You can avoid hardships by knowing the regulations and concerns of the park, monitoring weather conditions, traveling outside of the times of highest use, visiting in small groups when possible, and using a map and compass to ensure you don't have to make additions like cairns or other markers to find your way.

TRAVEL AND CAMP ON DURABLE SURFACES

Although Rocky Mountain National Park has specific rules about the distance your backcountry campsite must be from roads and trails, they also expect that you will camp on durable surfaces free of vegetation. Almost all the routes in this guide use formal trails for their entire length, but those trails often travel through alpine areas where vegetation is fragile and can't withstand even a few people stepping on them in a week's time. Tread lightly by always staying on the trail, even if you have to step into a puddle or hop across rocks.

DISPOSE OF WASTE PROPERLY

Please put all trash and other refuse into the appropriate receptacle. Rocky Mountain National Park provides trash receptacles at nearly all formal trailheads. You are responsible for carrying out everything you bring in with you. The one exception here is poop, which you should bury in a 6- to 8-inch-deep (15- to 20-cm-deep) cat hole. Pack out your toilet paper in a plastic bag. It takes longer than you might think for toilet paper to biodegrade in mountain climates, and animals will dig the paper up and scatter it around the landscape.

MINIMIZE CAMPFIRE IMPACTS

Given how dry this environment is and how destructive wildfires are in the Mountain West, you can have a fire only in designated campfire rings. Try to keep your fire small so that sparks don't drift off into dry brush. Make sure your fire is dead out, and scatter the ashes around to allow them to cool thoroughly.

RESPECT WILDLIFE

Respecting wildlife is actually a formal law in Rocky Mountain National Park. Visitors are prohibited from handling or bothering wildlife in any way, and you should attempt to keep at least 75 feet (23 m) between yourself and any wild animal you encounter. In addition, feeding such creatures alters their behaviors and can make them aggressive. It can lead to injuries, and in some cases, the park may be forced to euthanize the aggressive animal.

A sign marks the start of the Sprague Lake Nature Trail, a 1-mile loop that's wheelchair-friendly and good for families too (Hike 3).

BE CONSIDERATE OF OTHER VISITORS

A good rule of thumb here is to remember that every person you cross paths with on the trail spent a lot of time, money, and effort to get to the same place. They are all trying to enjoy their trip, and therefore you should extend whatever courtesy is reasonably within your power to ensure that you don't wreck someone else's experience. Specifically, this principle asks that you yield to others on the trail to reduce conflict and let the sounds of nature prevail. This includes not playing music out loud through your phone or your Bluetooth speakers. Not everybody wants to hear music on the trail; so out of respect, use headphones.

SAFETY

Hiking is, in general, a safe activity, but of course brings with it more hazards than a walk to your neighborhood coffee shop. Yes, Rocky Mountain National Park is a "park," but the more important word in its name is *mountain*, and as a sign on the Flattop Mountain Trail (Hike 13) bluntly states, "mountains don't care."

ALTITUDE SICKNESS

Altitude sickness can have many symptoms, including headaches, nausea, shortness of breath, dizziness, indigestion—and it can be very serious or just slightly annoying. A few things you can do to prevent it: drink enough water (probably more than you think you need), consume enough calories and electrolytes as you're drinking all that water, show up in good physical condition, and don't ascend too quickly. If you travel to the park from a lower elevation, it's good to allow your body a day to acclimatize a bit—for example, if you fly into Denver from sea level, arrive in Estes Park in the early afternoon, and try to charge up to Chasm Lake (elevation 11,800 feet/3597 m) in the same day, you probably won't feel very well by the end of the day.

THUNDERSTORMS

During the summer in Colorado, afternoon thunderstorms roll in almost like clockwork and pose a real danger at high altitudes. The best way to avoid being struck by lightning in the mountains is to avoid being any place lightning can find you—check weather forecasts before you head out, watch

Stone steps are a feature of the trail to Calypso Cascades and Ouzel Falls (Hike 20).

the sky for building clouds, and if clouds are building into a storm, get below tree line (or better yet, into your car). If you're planning a hike above tree line, get an early-morning start and plan to be heading down by noon. And bring a rain jacket, unless the weather forecast calls for zero percent chance of precipitation. As a fellow climber jokingly told me once during a rain shower, a forecast of a 40 percent chance of rain just means it's going to rain 40 percent of the day.

SUN EXPOSURE

Sunburns, to put it bluntly, are for amateurs. Yes, there is snow in the mountains all summer, and mountain winds can make it feel like early winter even when the sun is out, but that doesn't mean you won't get sunburned. The thinner atmosphere of Rocky Mountain National Park's high elevation means you're exposed to more UV radiation, and spending a day out in the mountains without wearing sunscreen is a good way to get a sunburn.

COLD

Even when it's 75 degrees Fahrenheit and sunny in Estes Park, it can be winter temperatures at higher altitudes. In general, you can expect a 3-degree drop in temperature for every 1000 feet (305 m) of elevation you ascend, and even more if there's any wind. Bring more layers than you think you need, even if you're not planning on being outside for very long. As the saying goes, "There's no bad weather, only bad clothing."

STEEP DROP-OFFS

Most of the hikes in this book avoid lots of exposure to large, steep drop-offs, but be aware that even a short fall on a switchback, or down a brief steep section of trail, can be very dangerous. If you fall on a hike, you're very likely going to land on something hard and angular—it's not like the ball pit at Chuck E. Cheese. Be aware of your environment and watch your step, especially when you're fatigued and it's extra easy to catch a toe on a rock or a tree root sticking out of the trail.

NAVIGATION CHALLENGES

The hikes in this book are mostly on well-established trails, and, as a rule, should not present navigational challenges. In

OPPOSITE: *The forest along the Eugenia Mine Trail (Hike 22)*

cases where a trail crosses a section of rock, talus, or a boulder field, or is otherwise more challenging to follow, look for cairns to guide you, or for deadfall or rocks lining the sides of a trail. Always carry a map and compass—and know how to use them. In addition, a smartphone app that works offline, such as Gaia GPS, can answer the question, "Are we on the right path?" in seconds. Just be sure you have downloaded the proper map before setting out on your hike, since there's often no cell service in many parts of the park.

WILDFIRES

As in many places across the western United States, wildfires have been increasing in breadth and destruction in Colorado the past several years. Some recent fires have burned portions of Rocky Mountain National Park and may affect some of the trails described in this book. As part of your trip or hike planning, check with the park (see Contacts) for current trail conditions. And while you're in the park, be careful not to start a new fire and, of course, always follow regulations and restrictions for campfires, whether you're car camping or traveling into the backcountry.

THE TEN ESSENTIALS

The Ten Essentials, originated by The Mountaineers, are particular items necessary to answer two crucial questions: Can you prevent emergencies and respond positively should one occur? And can you safely spend a night—or more—outside? This list is a starting point to guide you in preparation for your Rocky Mountain National Park adventure.

1. **Navigation:** The five fundamentals are a map, altimeter, compass, GPS device, and a personal locator beacon or other device to contact emergency first responders. (Note that smartphone apps can provide the first four, but battery-powered devices are known to fail.)

2. **Headlamp:** A light source that is not your smartphone will help you find your way in darkness should you run out of daylight. Bring spare batteries.

3. **Sun protection:** Wear sunglasses and sun-protective clothes, and use a broad-spectrum sunscreen rated at least SPF 30.

4. **First aid:** Basics include bandages; skin closures; gauze pads and dressings; roller bandage or wrap; tape; antiseptic; blister prevention and treatment supplies; nitrile gloves; tweezers; needle; nonprescription painkillers; antiinflammatory, anti-diarrheal, and antihistamine tablets; topical antibiotic; and any important personal prescriptions, including an EpiPen if you are allergic to insect bites and stings.

5. **Knife:** Also consider a multitool, strong tape, some cordage, and gear repair supplies.

6. **Fire:** Carry at least one butane lighter (or waterproof matches) and firestarter, such as chemical heat tabs, cotton balls soaked in petroleum jelly, or commercially prepared firestarter.

7. **Shelter:** In addition to a rain shell, carry a single-use bivy sack, plastic tube tent, or jumbo plastic trash bag.

8. **Extra food:** For shorter trips a one-day supply is reasonable.

9. **Extra water:** Carry sufficient water and have the skills and tools required to obtain and purify additional water.

10. **Extra clothes:** Pack additional layers needed to survive the night in the worst conditions that your party may realistically encounter.

HOW TO USE THIS GUIDE

The hikes in this book cover as much of the diverse environments of Rocky Mountain National Park as possible, from relaxed walks on flat paths at the bottom of mountain valleys, to all-day quad-busting climbs up steep trails into the thin air above 12,000 feet (3658 m). This collection of hikes is intended to provide a sampler menu of the best the park has to offer so that you can use it to decide how to spend your time while visiting.

Each of the trail descriptions in this guide contains encapsulated information about the route, a "notes" section containing information specific to a given route, brief highlights of the route, directions to the route via car and public transit (where available), a narrative describing how to follow a given route, and, when appropriate, suggestions on how to extend your hike.

All **distances**, **elevation gains**, and **high points** were derived from GPS data collected during fieldwork and through Caltopo.com and Strava.com. This information is presented in the English system (miles, feet), as well as the metric system (kilometers, meters). All distances except for high points are rounded up to the nearest tenth of a mile or tenth of a kilometer. Please note that due to the inherent variability of GPS data, your mileage may vary from what's presented here.

OPPOSITE: *A view between rock formations along the Tundra Communities Trail (Hike 27)*

There are three separate ratings for **Difficulty:** easy, medium, and hard. These ratings are intended for an average hiker with solid fitness and some hiking experience. The difficulty rating is generally based on the amount of mileage and elevation gain, and is a broad category—you may find that one hike with a "medium" rating feels much harder than another with the same rating. The elevation gain of a hike is probably a more important piece of information than the difficulty rating—for instance, a hike with 1200 feet (366 m) of elevation gain is roughly equivalent to climbing (and descending) 120 flights of stairs—worth considering when planning your day.

Easy: Short, family-friendly hikes that nearly all hikers can finish comfortably in less than an hour. Approximately 0.8 to 1.8 miles (1.3 km to 2.9 km) and up to 250 feet (76 m) of elevation gain.

Medium: Longer hikes that most reasonably fit hikers can complete between 1.5 and 5 hours. Approximately 3.2 to 8.8 miles (5.2 km to 14.2 km) and up to 1900 feet (580 m) of elevation gain.

Hard: Half-day to full-day hikes for experienced hikers, possibly involving scrambling, elevations higher than 12,000 feet (3658 m), steep slopes, and significant time above tree line. Approximately 7.2 to 14.8 miles (11.6 km to 23.8 km), and up to 4850 feet (1478 m) of elevation gain.

The **Maps** section references the appropriate USGS 7.5-minute topographic map or maps, as well as the National Geographic Trails Illustrated Map 200: Rocky Mountain National Park map. In general, since all the hikes in this book use well-established trails, and the hikes that travel off-trail are on talus or involve rock scrambling, a general map like the National Geographic Trails Illustrated map is sufficient. But if you'd like more detailed topographic data, you can purchase the USGS 7.5-minute topographic maps directly from www.usgs.gov/products/maps/topo-maps. As an alternative: The

MAP LEGEND

〔34〕	US highway	◓	Viewpoint
〔7〕	State highway	▲	Summit
——	Surface road	▪	Building or landmark
= = = = =	Unpaved road	)(	Pass
- - - - -	Hiking route	——	River or stream
- - - - -	Other trail	=	Waterfall
←	Direction of travel	▢	Lake
Ⓢ	Start	▢	Glacier
Ⓟ	Parking	⟱	Wetland/marsh
ⓟ	Alternate parking	▬	National Park
⊕	Picnic area	▬	National Forest
⛰	Campground		

website Caltopo.com is a superb online resource that allows you to customize topographic maps specifically for your hike. In addition to a paper map and compass, I recommend a smartphone app like Gaia GPS, which enables you to download sections of topo maps and access them, as well as your position, while hiking, even when your phone is in airplane mode (there is zero cell service in most of the park).

You will also find **GPS** coordinates for the location of each trailhead, based on the WGS 84 datum. These coordinates are listed in the decimal degree form because that is the easiest way to enter the coordinates into websites and applications like Google Maps.

Notes include specific information related to terrain or navigation; whether there's a restroom at the trailhead; whether fishing is allowed in lakes, rivers, or creeks on the hike; or any other unique quality that merits mention.

In the **Getting There** section you will find driving directions, usually from the Estes Park Visitor Center in Estes Park,

since the vast majority of park visitors stay somewhere on the east side of the park, and most of the hikes in this book are best accessed from the east side of the park. Some of the hikes on the west side of the park have driving directions from both the Estes Park Visitor Center and from the Kawuneeche Visitor Center, on the park's west side near the Grand Lake Entrance. When applicable, transit options are also included.

Within each hike, you will find a summary describing the specific features that make it noteworthy. **On the Trail** contains point-A-to-point-B directions and descriptions of other notable features you'll need to know in order to complete and enjoy the hikes. **Going Farther** allows you to extend your route to nearby destinations. In some cases, this refers to alternate return routes or approaches.

A NOTE ABOUT SAFETY

Safety is an important concern in all outdoor activities. No guidebook can alert you to every hazard or anticipate the limitations of every reader. Therefore, the descriptions of roads, trails, routes, and natural features in this book are not representations that a particular place or excursion will be safe for your party. When you follow any of the routes described in this book, you assume responsibility for your own safety. Under normal conditions, such excursions require the usual attention to traffic, road and trail conditions, weather, terrain, the capabilities of your party, and other factors. Keeping informed on current conditions and exercising common sense are the keys to a safe, enjoyable outing.

—*Mountaineers Books*

OPPOSITE: *Ferns and berries line portions of the trail to Fern Lake (Hike 9).*

BEAR LAKE ROAD

The corridor accessed via Bear Lake Road holds the densest concentration of hikes in this book, offering everything from ADA-accessible and family-friendly paths to alpine summits. This is one of the most popular areas in the park, easily reachable by either a short drive from the town of Estes Park or via the hiker shuttle system departing from the Estes Park Visitor Center. The draw to this area is both variety and up-close views of alpine lakes and dramatic peaks, both reachable in hikes from 1 mile (1.6 km) in length to 10 miles (16.1 km). Wildlife in the area ranges from the elk that congregate at just over 8000 feet (2438 m) elevation in the Moraine Park area in early fall to the marmots and pika that roam the alpine tundra at around 12,000 feet (3658 m) on Flattop Mountain.

This area includes six different trailheads, arrayed along the length of Bear Lake Road, and a diverse lineup of hikes, but almost all of the hikes in this area provide a view of the peaks of the Continental Divide—the same set of mountains you'll see arriving in Estes Park from the east, or from driving around town. This area is popular for good reason, and the biggest challenge in high season can be finding a parking spot, so plan on arriving early or utilizing the park's Park & Ride shuttle to access trailheads.

OPPOSITE: *Looking north down into Glacier Gorge along Glacier Creek from just below Black Lake (Hike 12)*

1 BEAR LAKE

Distance: 0.8 mile (1.3 km)
Elevation gain: 50 feet (15 m)
High point: 9490 feet (2893 m)
Difficulty: Easy
Trail surface: Packed dirt
Maps: USGS McHenrys Peak, National Geographic Trails Illustrated Map 200: Rocky Mountain National Park
GPS: 40.311869°, −105.645121°
Notes: High altitude; be aware of exposure to afternoon thunderstorms; toilet at trailhead; fishing prohibited

> A mellow, stroller-friendly walking path loops around a tree-lined alpine lake with views of surrounding peaks. A great introduction to the high-altitude environment of Rocky Mountain National Park.

GETTING THERE

Driving: From the Estes Park Visitor Center, turn left (west) onto US Highway 34 (Big Thompson Avenue) and drive 0.2 mile (0.3 km), merging onto US 36 (Elkhorn Avenue) for 0.4 mile (0.6 km). Turn left to stay on US 36 and follow it west for 3.8 miles (6.1 km) into Rocky Mountain National Park, through the Beaver Meadows Entrance Station. About 1000 feet (305 m) past the entrance station, turn left onto Bear Lake Road and follow it for 9.4 miles (15.1 km) to the Bear Lake Trailhead parking lot at the end of the road.

Transit: Drive to the RMNP Park & Ride lot on Bear Lake Road (5.1 miles/8.2 km from US 36; see driving directions above) and take the Bear Lake Route shuttle bus to the Bear Lake Trailhead, about a 10-minute ride from the Park & Ride lot. Or take the Hiker Shuttle Express bus from the Estes Park Visitor Center, then take the Bear Lake Route shuttle bus to the Bear Lake Trailhead.

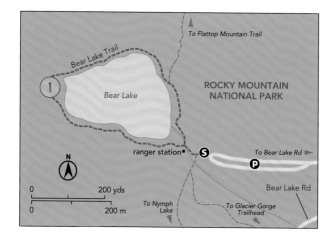

ON THE TRAIL

Because of its views, large parking lot, easy grade, proximity to Estes Park, accessibility, abundance of benches, and short length, the Bear Lake Trail is many visitors' first-ever hike at Rocky Mountain National Park (some while riding in strollers). If you were to choose a place to walk on your last-ever visit here late in life, it'd be hard to argue against picking this trail. All its attributes, of course, make it very popular, so if you're looking for solitude, it's best to show up very early in the morning, just before sunset, or when the weather is bad.

The trail is wide and very flat, and the packed dirt has very few roots and rocks to trip up feet or impede wheels of strollers or wheelchairs. The loop trail is ADA accessible for a few hundred feet in each direction from the parking lot, but a few sections where the trail grade steepens to more than 5 percent (and in some sections, 14 and 16 percent) keep it from being fully ADA accessible.

A brochure for a self-guided interpretive hike is available for a small fee at the Bear Lake Ranger Station kiosk at the trailhead—to follow the brochure, you'll want to proceed

A bench along the Bear Lake Trail invites hikers to enjoy views of Longs Peak.

counterclockwise on the trail around the lake. If you're not doing the interpretive hike, head in either direction. No matter which direction you choose, you'll stroll through lodgepole pines, see aspens (their leaves turn golden and light up the hillside for a few weeks in the fall), and pass by large granite boulders. Enjoy views of Hallett Peak rising above the southwest edge of the lake and, to the southeast, Longs Peak, Pagoda Mountain, and the spires of the Keyboard of the Winds between Longs and Pagoda. Two other trails intersect with the Bear Lake Trail—remain on the fork nearest to the lake to stay on the loop trail.

2 ALBERTA FALLS

Distance: 1.8 miles (2.9 km)
Elevation gain: 250 feet (76 m)
High point: 9400 feet (2865 m)
Difficulty: Easy
Trail surface: Dirt, rock
Maps: USGS McHenrys Peak, National Geographic Trails Illustrated Map 200: Rocky Mountain National Park
GPS: 40.310567°, –105.640202°
Notes: High altitude; be aware of exposure to afternoon thunderstorms; toilet at trailhead

This short, popular, family-friendly hike with a bit of elevation gain leads to a stunning three-story-high alpine waterfall.

GETTING THERE

Driving: From the Estes Park Visitor Center, turn left (west) onto US Highway 34 (Big Thompson Avenue) and drive 0.2 mile (0.3 km), merging onto US 36 (Elkhorn Avenue) for 0.4 mile (0.6 km). Turn left to stay on US 36 and follow it west for 3.8 miles (6.1 km) into Rocky Mountain National Park, through the Beaver Meadows Entrance Station. About 1000 feet (305 m) past the entrance station, turn left onto Bear Lake Road and follow it for 8.3 miles (13.4 km), turning left into the Glacier Gorge Trailhead parking lot. Note: Parking here is very limited.

Transit: Drive to the RMNP Park & Ride lot on Bear Lake Road (5.1 miles/8.2 km from US 36; see driving directions above) and take the Bear Lake Route shuttle bus to the Glacier Gorge Trailhead, about a 10-minute ride from the Park & Ride lot. Or take the Hiker Shuttle Express bus from the Estes Park Visitor Center, then take the Bear Lake Route shuttle bus to the Glacier Gorge Trailhead.

ON THE TRAIL

The trail heads southwest out of the parking lot, then winds through an evergreen forest with a handful of aspens, dotted with large boulders. At the first trail junction, about 0.25 mile (0.4 km) from the trailhead parking lot, stay straight (right).

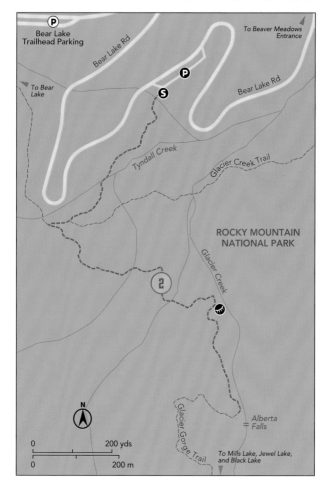

The cascades of Alberta Falls

Reach a signed junction at 0.3 mile (0.5 km)—head left, following the sign to Alberta Falls.

At 0.6 mile (1 km), you'll be able to hear, and then see from a viewpoint to the left of the trail, the waters of Glacier Creek rushing downhill. The creek roughly parallels nearby Bear Creek Road for a couple of miles before it joins the Big Thompson River just west of Estes Park, then flows through town and into Lake Estes. Alberta Falls is just uphill from you now—follow the trail for another 0.3 (0.5 km) mile to the three-story-high waterfall.

During the busy season, you might not have the waterfall to yourself, but if you scramble around on the rocks a bit, you can usually find a spot to sit and enjoy it. The water rushing down in front of you was very recently snowmelt on the peaks surrounding Glacier Gorge, upstream from Alberta Falls: Longs Peak, Pagoda Mountain, Chiefs Head Peak, McHenrys Peak, and Arrowhead. The water first fills Black Lake below the peaks before traveling downstream to Jewel Lake and Mills Lake, then drops another few hundred feet to the top of Alberta Falls.

GOING FARTHER

The Glacier Gorge Trail continues beyond Alberta Falls: head up the gorge to Mills Lake (Hike 4), hiking 2 miles (3.2 km) and 560 vertical feet (170 m) farther past the falls; or trek to Jewel Lake, located 2.25 miles (3.6 km) beyond the falls (same elevation as Mills Lake); or climb up to Black Lake (Hike 12), at 4 miles (6.4 km) and 1240 vertical feet (378 m) farther than the falls.

3   SPRAGUE LAKE

Distance: **0.8 mile (1.3 km)**
Elevation gain: **Negligible**
High point: **8690 feet (2649 m)**
Difficulty: **Easy**
Trail surface: **Packed gravel**
Maps: USGS Longs Peak, National Geographic Trails Illustrated Map 200: Rocky Mountain National Park
GPS: 40.320468°, –105.607776°
Notes: High altitude; be aware of exposure to afternoon thunderstorms; toilet at trailhead; catch-and-keep fishing

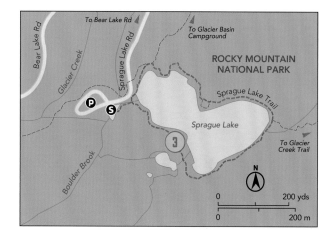

A flat, ADA-accessible path circles a quiet lake, with views of the high peaks of the Continental Divide and opportunities for fishing.

GETTING THERE

Driving: From the Estes Park Visitor Center, turn left (west) onto US Highway 34 (Big Thompson Avenue) and drive 0.2 mile (0.3 km), merging onto US 36 (Elkhorn Avenue) for 0.4 mile (0.6 km). Turn left to stay on US 36 and follow it west for 3.8 miles (6.1 km) into Rocky Mountain National Park, through the Beaver Meadows Entrance Station. About 1000 feet (305 m) past the entrance station, turn left onto Bear Lake Road and follow it for 5.8 miles. Turn left (south) onto Sprague Lake Road, and drive for 0.1 mile (0.2 km), turning right at the T intersection to stay on Sprague Lake Road for the final 0.2 mile (0.3 km) to the parking lot.

Transit: Drive to the RMNP Park & Ride lot on Bear Lake Road (5.1 miles/8.2 km from US 36; see driving directions above) and take the Moraine Park Route shuttle bus to Sprague Lake/Glacier Creek Stables, about a 5-minute ride

A view of Sprague Lake in the early evening

from the Park & Ride lot. Or take the Hiker Shuttle Express bus from the Estes Park Visitor Center, then take the Moraine Park Route shuttle bus to Sprague Lake/Glacier Creek Stables.

ON THE TRAIL

Sprague Lake is one of the best places in Rocky Mountain National Park to watch a sunrise. As the sun pops up over the horizon, it paints the peaks on the Continental Divide a glowing pink for a few minutes. And the trail here is so flat and wide that it's easy to carry a full mug of coffee along without spilling it. Bring a headlamp or flashlight, and time it so you can stand somewhere on the northeast side of the lake as the sun comes up, and you'll head home with at least one great photo: the calm lake, thick stands of trees behind it, and the glowing mountains above.

That said, you don't have to get out of bed early to enjoy this hike. It's fully ADA accessible, stroller- and kid-friendly, low-commitment, and has tons of wildflowers and fishing spots (mostly brook trout and rainbow trout). There's even an ADA-accessible backcountry campsite past the east end of the lake (advance reservation required). The trail is a loop around the lake, and can be walked in either direction—but if you're in a hurry to get to the view of the mountains for sunrise, go clockwise.

Sprague Lake is a remnant of tourism efforts that occurred just before Rocky Mountain National Park was established: Abner Sprague, who operated a lodge here from 1914 to 1940 with his wife, Alberta, built a dam at the east end of the lake to enlarge the lake so guests at the lodge, which stood where today's parking lot is located, could have better fishing. Sprague, who lived to be ninety-one, climbed Longs Peak in 1874, and again at age seventy-four in 1924, fifty years after his first climb.

During the summer and early fall, more than twenty species of wildflowers can be seen along the Sprague Lake Trail, including yarrow, Rocky Mountain goldenrod, blanketflowers, glacial daisies, and fireweed.

A TUNNEL UNDER THE MOUNTAINS

The Alva B. Adams Tunnel, part of the largest transmountain water diversion in Colorado, runs 13.1 miles (21.1 km) in a straight line under the Continental Divide in Rocky Mountain National Park, moving water from the Colorado River to Colorado's Front Range. At one point, the tunnel is 3800 feet (1158 m) below the surface of the mountains. It was completed in 1944 and named after Senator Alva B. Adams, who fought for the tunnel but did not live to see it finished. The tunnel is 10 feet (3 m) in diameter and is marked on the official NPS park map.

4 MILLS LAKE

Distance: 5.6 miles (9 km)
Elevation gain: 780 feet (238 m)
High point: 9940 feet (3030 m)
Difficulty: Medium
Trail surface: Dirt, rock
Maps: USGS McHenrys Peak, National Geographic Trails Illustrated Map 200: Rocky Mountain National Park
GPS: 40.310567°, −105.640202°
Notes: High altitude; be aware of exposure to afternoon thunderstorms; toilet at trailhead; catch-and-keep fishing

> A lunch spot with a view of the Keyboard of the Winds—a group of dramatic spires on the southwest ridge of Longs Peak—and the peak itself, Mills Lake give this day hike a high ratio of reward per mile.

GETTING THERE

Driving: From the Estes Park Visitor Center, turn left (west) onto US Highway 34 (Big Thompson Avenue) and drive 0.2 mile (0.3 km), merging onto US 36 (Elkhorn Avenue) for 0.4 mile (0.6 km). Turn left to stay on US 36 and follow it west for 3.8 miles (6.1 km) into Rocky Mountain National Park, through the Beaver Meadows Entrance Station. About 1000 feet (305 m) past the entrance station, turn left onto Bear Lake Road and follow it for 8.3 miles (13.4 km), turning left into the Glacier Gorge Trailhead parking lot. Note: Parking here is very limited.

Transit: Drive to the RMNP Park & Ride lot on Bear Lake Road (5.1 miles/8.2 km from US 36; see driving directions above) and take the Bear Lake Route shuttle bus to the Glacier Gorge Trailhead, about a 10-minute ride from the Park & Ride lot. Or take the Hiker Shuttle Express bus from the Estes

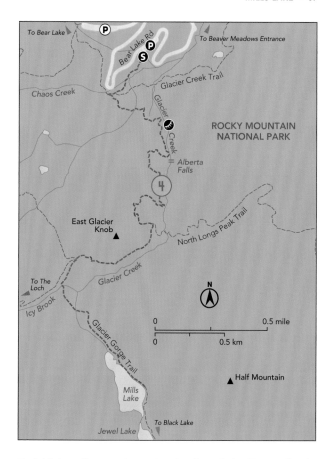

Park Visitor Center, then take the Bear Lake Route shuttle bus to the Glacier Gorge Trailhead.

ON THE TRAIL

The trail heads southwest out of the parking lot, then winds through an evergreen forest with a handful of aspens, dotted with large boulders. At the first trail junction, about 0.25 mile

(0.4 km) from the trailhead parking lot, stay straight (right). At 0.3 mile (0.5 km), reach a signed trail junction—head left, following the sign to Alberta Falls.

At 0.6 mile (1 km), you hear, and then can see from a viewpoint to the left of the trail, the waters of Glacier Creek rushing downhill. The creek roughly parallels nearby Bear Creek Road for a couple of miles before it joins the Big Thompson River just west of Estes Park, then flows through town and into Lake Estes. Alberta Falls is just uphill from you now; follow the trail for another 0.3 mile (0.5 km) to the three-story-high waterfall.

During the busy season, you might not have the waterfall to yourself, but if you scramble around on the rocks a bit, you can usually find a spot to sit and enjoy it. The water rushing down in front of you was very recently snowmelt on the peaks surrounding Glacier Gorge, upstream from Alberta Falls: Longs Peak, Pagoda Mountain, Chiefs Head Peak, McHenrys Peak, and Arrowhead. The water first fills Black Lake below the peaks before traveling downstream to Jewel Lake and Mills Lake, then dropping another few hundred feet to the top of Alberta Falls.

After Alberta Falls, you have more solitude as the majority of hikers will stop at the three-story-high waterfall and not continue farther—fortunate for you, but unfortunate for them.

The trail continues a gradual climb through thinning evergreen forest, passing the junction with the North Longs Peak Trail at 1.5 miles where you want to stay south/right. At the 1.6-mile (2.6 km) mark, the trail turns a corner to go south/southwest around the base of East Glacier Knob, one of two lumps of rock that rise about 400 feet (122 m) above the trail at the north end of Glacier Gorge. The turn in the trail presents an open preview of the alpine scenery you're headed toward. It's also at this point that you get an indication of

OPPOSITE: *Mills Lake as seen from its north end*

the weather above in Glacier Gorge for the day: if it's going to be cold and windy, you'll get an abrupt blast of air in the face as you turn the corner. Not necessarily a sign you should turn back, but definitely a sign of what the temperature will be like at Mills Lake, a little more than a mile (1.6 km) up the trail and 200 feet (61 m) higher.

At the trail junction at 2 miles (3.2 km), continue left on the Glacier Gorge Trail to reach Mills Lake—heading straight will take you toward The Loch (Hike 5), a great day hike as well (and a 1.5-mile/2.4-km roundtrip detour on your way back, if you'd like). Just after the trail junction, cross Icy Brook, then Glacier Creek, and a few hundred feet farther, your route skirts the north edge of Mills Lake, where you can take a break and enjoy the view. The 1500-foot-long (457-m-long) lake spans the bottom of Glacier Gorge, at the base of sweeping walls carpeted with conifers. On the left-hand (east) skyline above the lake, you can see the west face of Longs Peak (14,259 feet/4346 m), and to its right the towers of the Keyboard of the Winds (hopefully you won't have enough wind to find out how they got their name—from the noise they make when high winds rake across them). Further to the right you'll see the long North Buttress of Pagoda Mountain (13,497 feet/4114 m), Chiefs Head Peak (13,579 feet/4139 m), and just in front of and below Chiefs Head, the pointed Spearhead (12,575 feet/3833 m).

There's a small rock peninsula at the north end of Mills Lake just large enough for four or five people to sit on, and if you're lucky to find it unoccupied, it makes a great spot for lunch and photos before you return the way you came.

GOING FARTHER

In addition to the aforementioned potential detour to The Loch, you can also continue up the Glacier Gorge Trail to Jewel Lake (0.25 mile/0.4 km farther) or to Black Lake (2 miles/3.2 km and 700 vertical feet/213 m farther; Hike 12).

5 THE LOCH

Distance: 5.8 miles (9.3 km)
Elevation gain: 1000 feet (305 m)
High point: 10,180 feet (3103 m)
Difficulty: Medium
Trail surface: Dirt, rock
Maps: USGS McHenrys Peak, National Geographic Trails Illustrated Map 200: Rocky Mountain National Park
GPS: 40.310567°, −105.640202°
Notes: High altitude; be aware of exposure to afternoon thunderstorms; toilet at trailhead; limited parking; catch-and-keep fishing

A short but steep out-and-back hike reaches a lake with expansive views of an alpine cirque, with a stop at 30-foot high Alberta Falls along the way.

GETTING THERE

Driving: From the Estes Park Visitor Center, turn left (west) onto US Highway 34 (Big Thompson Avenue) and drive 0.2 mile (0.3 km), merging onto US 36 (Elkhorn Avenue) for 0.4 mile (0.6 km). Turn left to stay on US 36 and follow it west for 3.8 miles (6.1 km) into Rocky Mountain National Park, through the Beaver Meadows Entrance Station. About 1000 feet (305 m) past the entrance station, turn left onto Bear Lake Road and follow it for 8.3 miles (13.4 km), turning left into the Glacier Gorge Trailhead parking lot.

Transit: Drive to the RMNP Park & Ride lot on Bear Lake Road (5.1 miles/8.2 km from US 36; see driving directions above) and take the Bear Lake Route shuttle bus to the Glacier Gorge Trailhead, about a 10-minute ride from the Park & Ride lot. Or take the Hiker Shuttle Express bus from the Estes Park Visitor Center, then take the Bear Lake Route shuttle bus to the Glacier Gorge Trailhead.

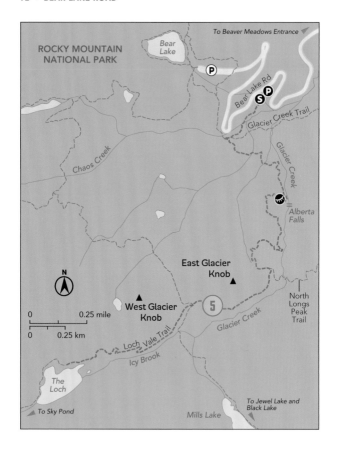

ON THE TRAIL

From the Glacier Gorge Trailhead, the trail winds through an evergreen forest with a handful of aspens, dotted with large boulders. At 0.3 mile (0.5 km), you'll reach a signed trail junction—head left, following the sign to Loch Vale. Here, the trail begins steadily climbing with only a few breaks.

At 0.9 mile (1.5 km), you'll pass by the viewpoint for Alberta Falls (Hike 2), where Glacier Creek drops three stories on its way to the Big Thompson River a few miles away. From here, the trail continues to wind and climb, at 1.4 miles (2.3 km) heading toward the high north wall of East Glacier Knob before curving around its southeast side. At 1.5 miles (2.4 km), the trail intersects the North Longs Peak Trail—stay right, following the sign to Loch Vale. The trail grade eases a bit here, and around the corner the view opens up to West Glacier Knob and Thatchtop Mountain.

At the four-way trail junction at 2 miles (3.2 km), take the middle fork, following the sign for Loch Vale. The trail steepens a bit here, climbing the last 400 feet (122 m) to The Loch in the last mile, traversing the gorge above Icy Brook. At 2.5 miles (4 km), the trail switchbacks and takes you away from the creek for the rest of the climb. At 2.8 miles (4.5 km), you'll arrive at the far east end of The Loch, a vibrant blue-green alpine lake that, when still, can reflect the mountains above it. If you opt to fish, you might catch greenback cutthroat

The Loch with Taylor Peak behind

trout and brook trout. A signed trail goes right around the north side of The Loch, up to Sky Pond and Andrews Glacier, and an unmarked trail heads left to a rock peninsula and a 180-degree view of The Loch and the dramatic cirque behind it.

To return to the trailhead, head back the way you came, following signs to Glacier Gorge Trailhead.

6 ODESSA LAKE VIA BEAR LAKE TRAILHEAD

Distance: 8.8 miles (14.2 km)
Elevation gain: 1900 feet (579 m)
High point: 10,685 feet (3257 m)
Difficulty: Medium
Trail surface: Dirt, rock, talus
Maps: USGS McHenrys Peak, National Geographic Trails Illustrated Map 200: Rocky Mountain National Park
GPS: 40.311869°, −105.645121°
Notes: High altitude; be aware of exposure to afternoon thunderstorms; toilet at trailhead; catch-and-release fishing

This steadily climbing out-and-back hike provides somewhat delayed gratification—great views starting at the 3-mile mark and continuing to an alpine lake (with greenback cutthroat trout) that is less visited than most hikes reached from the Bear Lake Trailhead.

GETTING THERE

Driving: From the Estes Park Visitor Center, turn left (west) onto US Highway 34 (Big Thompson Avenue) and drive 0.2 mile (0.3 km), merging onto US 36 (Elkhorn Avenue) for 0.4 mile (0.6 km). Turn left to stay on US 36 and follow it west for 3.8 miles (6.1 km) into Rocky Mountain National

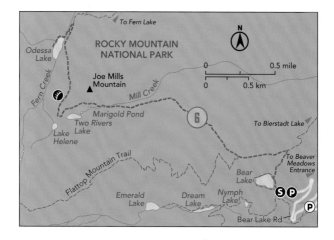

Park, through the Beaver Meadows Entrance Station. About 1000 feet (305 m) past the entrance station, turn left onto Bear Lake Road and follow it for 9.4 miles (15.1 km) to the Bear Lake Trailhead parking lot at the end of the road.

Transit: Drive to the RMNP Park & Ride lot on Bear Lake Road (5.1 miles/8.2 km from US 36; see driving directions above) and take the Bear Lake Route shuttle bus to the Bear Lake Trailhead, about a 10-minute ride from the Park & Ride lot. Or take the Hiker Shuttle Express bus from the Estes Park Visitor Center, then take the Bear Lake Route shuttle bus to the Bear Lake Trailhead.

ON THE TRAIL

From the Bear Lake Trailhead, walk across the short foot-bridge next to the ranger cabin and head right, toward Bear Lake. Turn right onto the wide path that circles Bear Lake, heading counterclockwise around the lake. At the junction at 0.1 mile (160 m), turn right, following the sign to Odessa Lake, starting to climb through aspens, pines, and boulders, up and away from the lake. At the 0.4-mile mark (0.6 km),

you'll reach another trail junction—take the left fork, following the sign to Odessa Lake. Continue climbing up a rocky trail with log and stone steps and views through the trees of Longs Peak, Glacier Gorge, and Otis Peak.

At the trail junction at 0.9 mile (1.5 km), turn right to follow the sign to Odessa Lake. From here, you'll flirt with the edge of tree line but keep gradually climbing, traversing the lower north slopes of Flattop Mountain through pines and wildflowers: heartleaf arnica, scarlet paintbrush, and Bigelow's tansyaster. At 1.6 miles (2.6 km), cross a series of five streams, and continue on a nice path through a large boulder field at mile 2.3 (3.7 km). Around mile 2.4 (3.9 km), you pass a couple small ponds on the left (south), and then the signed turnoff for the Sourdough backcountry campsite.

Continuing on, keep your eyes open for an unmarked trail junction around mile 3 (4.8 km), where a social trail leads up to the right, climbing about 20 feet (6 m) to a fantastic viewpoint on the southwest shoulder of Joe Mills Mountain that looks across the narrow valley below at Notchtop Mountain and Little Matterhorn, and below and to the north, Odessa Lake.

Return to the main trail, and at mile 3.1 (5 km), stay right at a junction with a social trail that leads to a pond on the left. Your trail begins to contour around Joe Mills Mountain, to traverse a half mile of scree fields before reentering the trees again just before the route descends to the lake (the trail through the scree fields may be covered in patches of snow in spots through June or July). Enjoy the 700-foot (213-m) descent as much as you can—you'll be climbing back up it on your way out.

At 4.2 miles (6.8 km), come to a junction with an easy-to-miss hairpin left turn leading to Odessa Lake. The trail runs parallel on the left side of a creek for about 200 feet (61 m)

OPPOSITE: *The trail along Fern Creek, just north of Odessa Lake, with Notchtop Mountain in the background*

before crossing the creek on a log bridge and continuing on the right side of the creek to the lake, at 4.4 miles (7.1 km). From the edge of the lake's shallow blue-green waters, enjoy views of Notchtop Mountain (12,129 feet/3697 m) and the Little Matterhorn (11,586 feet/3531 m), which looks more like the real Matterhorn from this side.

To return to the trailhead, reverse your steps, following signs to the Bear Lake Trailhead.

7 FOUR LAKES LOOP

Distance: **5.6 miles (9 km)**
Elevation gain: **1030 feet (314 m)**
High point: **10,220 feet (3115 m)**
Difficulty: **Medium**
Trail surface: **Dirt, rock, asphalt, some scrambling**
Maps: **USGS McHenrys Peak, National Geographic Trails Illustrated Map 200: Rocky Mountain National Park**
GPS: **40.311869°, −105.645121°**
Notes: **High altitude; be aware of exposure to afternoon thunderstorms; toilet at trailhead; fishing prohibited at Bear Lake**

A high reward-per-step ratio makes this hike a popular choice for a half day, packing in four distinct alpine lakes in less than 6 miles of hiking.

GETTING THERE

Driving: From the Estes Park Visitor Center, turn left (west) onto US Highway 34 (Big Thompson Avenue) and drive 0.2 mile (0.3 km), merging onto US 36 (Elkhorn Avenue) for 0.4 mile (0.6 km). Turn left to stay on US 36 and follow it west for 3.8 miles (6.1 km) into Rocky Mountain National Park, through the Beaver Meadows Entrance Station. About 1000

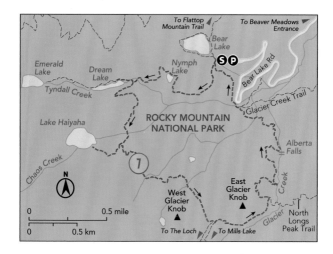

feet (305 m) past the entrance station, turn left onto Bear Lake Road and follow it for 9.4 miles (15.1 km) to the Bear Lake Trailhead parking lot at the end of the road.

Transit: Drive to the RMNP Park & Ride lot on Bear Lake Road (5.1 miles/8.2 km from US 36; see driving directions above) and take the Bear Lake Route shuttle bus to the Bear Lake Trailhead, about a 10-minute ride from the Park & Ride lot. Or take the Hiker Shuttle Express bus from the Estes Park Visitor Center, then take the Bear Lake Route shuttle bus to the Bear Lake Trailhead.

ON THE TRAIL

You can head right (northwest) and in about 100 feet (31 m) of walking, get a nice view of Bear Lake, or visit it later on your way back (and grab a seat on a bench to relax after completing the hike). To begin the Four Lakes Loop from the T intersection, follow signs pointing to Dream Lake, Nymph Lake, and Lake Haiyaha, to the left (south). The trail is paved with asphalt at first as it climbs, and after about 0.3 mile (0.5 km) turns to dirt and rock, just before passing a

Dream Lake framed by Hallett Peak and Flattop Mountain

small lily pond on the left (west)—this is Nymph Lake. The trail circles to the end of the lake, and then climbs between large boulders, and then up a series of log steps, climbing to a cascading creek on the left. Cross the creek on a wide wooden bridge, and after a few more steps (0.9 mile/1.5 km total) come to a trail junction. You'll take the right (north) fork for 0.1 mile (160 m) to the east end of Dream Lake. Dream Lake is a long alpine lake ringed with trees, and behind its far west end, you'll see Hallett Peak (12,713 feet/3875 m), and to its right, the jagged south face of Flattop Mountain (12,324 feet/3756 m). Dream Lake contains greenback and Colorado River cutthroat trout and is open to catch-and-release fishing using barbless hooks.

Retrace your steps 0.1 mile (160 m) to the last trail junction, and turn right (south), following the signs to Lake Haiyaha. Climb the steep, rocky trail up 300 vertical feet (91 m) in the next half mile, to increasingly more open views of Longs Peak and the Keyboard of the Winds, then drop down to cross a couple of streams, one on a bridge, one on rockwork. At the next trail junction, continue straight on the right fork, heading south and then west, following the sign to Lake Haiyaha. At 2 miles (3.2 km), the trail disappears into talus as you pass a small pond on the left (southwest). Follow your instincts and meander about 70 more feet (21 m) through the talus on the north side of the pond, possibly scrambling a little through the larger boulders, to the green waters and rocky shoreline of Lake Haiyaha where catch-and-keep fishing is allowed. The streaked southeast face of Hallett Peak dominates the skyline above.

Head back the way you came, to the last trail junction (2.3 miles/3.7 km). Take the right fork heading east and south, following the sign to the Loch-Mills junction. From here, the trail meanders downhill along a drainage, crossing several streams, then follows rockwork through forest, popping out onto rock slabs to pass by a small pond at mile 2.9 (4.7 km). Pass beneath a rock wall on the right, the northeast face of West Glacier Knob, until a trail junction at mile 3.4 (5.5 km). Take the far-left fork, following the sign to the Glacier Gorge Trailhead. As you walk around the southeast corner of East Glacier Knob, you'll come to another junction at 3.9 miles

(6.3 km). Stay straight (left), following the sign to the Glacier Gorge Trailhead. At 4.7 miles (7.6 km), you'll pass by Alberta Falls (Hike 2), a nice bonus in addition to your four lakes (if you'd like, you can refer to this as "The Four Lakes and a Waterfall Loop"). After the falls, the trail widens through aspens and pines as it approaches the Glacier Gorge Trailhead. At mile 5.2 (8.4 km), cross a shallow creek on a log bridge or by hopping the stones next to it, and 500 feet (152 m) later, reach a junction, taking the left (west) fork to head back uphill to the Bear Lake Trailhead.

GOING FARTHER

If you haven't quite gotten your fill of alpine lakes, plenty of options can be incorporated into this loop to make it longer, including The Loch (Hike 5), Mills Lake (Hike 4), or Black Lake (Hike 12).

8   CUB LAKE

Distance: 4.8 miles (7.7 km)
Elevation gain: 570 feet (174 m)
High point: 8670 feet (2643 m)
Difficulty: Medium
Trail surface: Dirt, rock
Maps: USGS McHenrys Peak, National Geographic Trails Illustrated Map 200: Rocky Mountain National Park
GPS: 40.356182°, –105.615773°
Notes: High altitude; be aware of exposure to afternoon thunderstorms; toilet at trailhead

This mellow lower-elevation hike traverses a meadow, forest, and a wildfire burn area that is now regrowing to end at a peaceful lake with a mountain backdrop.

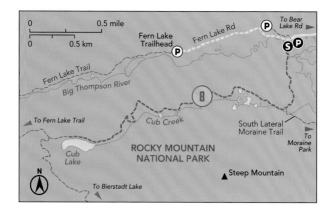

GETTING THERE

Driving: From the Estes Park Visitor Center, turn left (west) onto US Highway 34 (Big Thompson Avenue) and drive 0.2 mile (0.3 km), merging onto US 36 (Elkhorn Avenue) for 0.4 mile (0.6 km). Turn left to stay on US 36 and follow it west for 3.8 miles (6.1 km) into Rocky Mountain National Park, through the Beaver Meadows Entrance Station. About 1000 feet (305 m) past the entrance station, turn left onto Bear Lake Road and follow it for 1.3 miles (2.1 km), turning right (southwest) onto Moraine Park Road. Stay on Moraine Park Road for 0.5 mile (0.8 km), turning left (south) onto Fern Lake Road and following it for 1.3 miles (2.1 km) to the Cub Lake Trailhead on the left. If the lot is full, there are a couple of overflow lots about 800 feet (244 m) farther down Fern Lake Road.

Transit: Drive to the RMNP Park & Ride lot on Bear Lake Road (5.1 miles/8.2 km from US 36; see driving directions above) and take the Moraine Park Route shuttle bus to the Cub Lake Trailhead, about a 20-minute ride from the Park & Ride lot. Or take the Hiker Shuttle Express bus from the Estes Park Visitor Center, then take the Moraine Park Route shuttle bus to the Cub Lake Trailhead.

ON THE TRAIL

Cub Lake is not one of the most famous lakes in Rocky Mountain National Park (nor is it on the park's list of fishable lakes), but that's what makes it great (and less crowded). The trail's lower elevation and gentler grade enable hikers to see several distinct environments, from the valley floor of the Moraine Park, up through a dense forest, and ending at a lake with a view of the high-elevation peaks the park is famous for.

From the Cub Lake Trailhead, the trail heads south out of the parking lot, almost immediately crossing a wide bridge over the Big Thompson River—at this point, about 10 miles (16 km) downstream from its headwaters, it is a quite calm but wide stream. For the next half mile, the trail traces the west edge of the Moraine Park, a marshy area dotted with wildflowers and sagebrush, and in the fall, home to large herds of elk. During the first half of the 1900s, Moraine Park was home to Steads Ranch, a resort that included guest houses, a hotel, rodeo grounds, and a golf course. In the 1960s, the park purchased the property, removed the buildings, and reseeded the golf course with native grasses.

At the fork in the trail at about 0.6 mile (1 km), stay right (west), following the sign to Cub Lake and walk for almost a mile, contouring around the north edge of a series of grassy meadows at the base of 9538-foot (2907 m) Steep Mountain, directly to the south. Views of the Continental Divide open up here, and the mountain you see at the end of the valley is 12,922-foot (3939 m) Stones Peak. At about 1.5 miles (1.9 km), the trail begins to climb, traveling through a meadow and past a small pond. The steepest part of the trail is the last 0.75 mile (1.2 km), which becomes narrow and rocky as it climbs through dense old-growth aspens. At around 2.2 miles (3.5 km), the trail enters the remnants of the 2012 Fern Lake Fire, a wildfire started by an illegal campfire in October of that year that burned more than 3500 acres in just over two months until a snowstorm finally extinguished

Cub Lake from the northwest

it. Among the regrowth present, dense areas of purple wild bergamot flowers may be visible in the summer months.

At 2.4 miles (3.9 km), a spur trail leads off to the right (north) to the Cub Creek backcountry campsite—stay straight (west) here to continue to the lake. At 2.5 miles (4 km), you'll arrive at Cub Lake, which in the summer months will be studded with lily pads. The trail continues around the north side of the lake to other viewpoints and, eventually, junctions with other trails. To return to the trailhead, retrace your steps.

GOING FARTHER

It is possible to link the hike to Cub Lake with a trip to Fern Lake (Hike 9), adding another 2.5 miles (4 km) and 900 vertical feet (274 m) up.

9 FERN LAKE

Distance: 7.6 miles (12.2 km)
Elevation gain: 1400 feet (427 m)
High point: 9525 feet (2903 m)
Difficulty: Medium
Trail surface: Dirt, rock
Maps: USGS McHenrys Peak, National Geographic Trails Illustrated Map 200: Rocky Mountain National Park
GPS: 40.354886°, −105.631104°
Notes: High altitude; be aware of exposure to afternoon thunderstorms; toilet at trailhead; catch-and-release fishing with barbless hooks

This gradually steepening hike parallels the Big Thompson River, visits a 60-foot (18 m) waterfall, and then a lesser-visited alpine lake with mountain views.

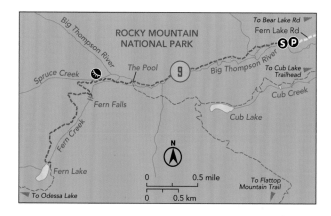

GETTING THERE

Driving: From the Estes Park Visitor Center, turn left (west) onto US Highway 34 (Big Thompson Avenue) and drive 0.2 mile (0.3 km), merging onto US 36 (Elkhorn Avenue) for 0.4 mile (0.6 km). Turn left to stay on US 36 and follow it west for 3.8 miles (6.1 km) into Rocky Mountain National Park, through the Beaver Meadows Entrance Station. About 1000 feet (305 m) past the entrance station, turn left onto Bear Lake Road and follow it for 1.3 miles (2.1 km), turning right (southwest) onto Moraine Park Road. Stay on Moraine Park Road for 0.5 mile (0.8 km), turning left (south) onto Fern Lake Road and following it for 2.2 miles (3.5 km) to the Fern Lake Trailhead parking lot at the end of the road.

Transit: Drive to the RMNP Park & Ride lot on Bear Lake Road (5.1 miles/8.2 km from US 36; see driving directions above) and take the Moraine Park Route shuttle bus to the Fern Lake Trailhead, about a 20-minute ride from the Park & Ride lot. Or take the Hiker Shuttle Express bus from the Estes Park Visitor Center, then take the Moraine Park Route shuttle bus to the Fern Lake Trailhead.

ON THE TRAIL

From the west end of the Fern Lake Trailhead parking lot, the trail runs parallel to the north of the Big Thompson River and under a set of cliffs to the south, at a very gentle grade for the first mile and a half. You'll pass through stands of aspens and pines with a lush understory of bracken ferns and, in season, wildflowers: cow parsnips, wild bergamot, and others.

At 1.2 miles (1.9 km), the trail passes by and through a number of large boulders, on some of which you may be able to spot climbers' chalk (hint: the chalk marks are not as high as you might think, since these are boulder problems—short but difficult climbing routes). At 1.4 miles (2.3 km), a spur trail leads off to the right (north) to the Arch Rocks backcountry campsite—continue straight here. At 1.7 miles (2.7 km), the trail crosses a bridge over the Big Thompson River at The Pool, and on the other side of the bridge, reaches a trail junction with the Cub Lake Trail. Take the right fork following the sign to Fern Falls and Fern Lake. The trail begins climbing in earnest now, starting up rock steps to views of the valley, in which you'll see signs of the 2012 Fern Lake Fire, a wildfire started by an illegal campfire in October of that year that burned more than 3500 acres in just over two months until a snowstorm finally extinguished it.

At 1.9 miles, you'll pass the turnoff for the Old Forest Inn campsite on the right (north), where the Forest Inn stood from 1917 until the park acquired and removed it in 1959. (Accommodations at the site nowadays are more DIY, but provide much more solitude.) A few hundred feet later, you'll cross a log bridge over Fern Creek, and then at 2.1 miles (3.4 km), the trail passes a viewpoint to the right (north), where you can take in the cascades of Spruce Creek. At this point, the trail climbs parallel to the two creeks, and for most of the summer until the flow of water slows, you hike with the sounds of both creeks rushing past, one in each ear.

OPPOSITE: *The bridge across the Big Thompson River at The Pool*

The trail continues to climb steeply through evergreen forest to Fern Falls, a six-story waterfall, at the 2.7-mile mark (4.4 km). Over the next 1.1 mile (1.8 km), the trail moves away from Spruce Creek and climbs more than 600 feet (183 m) before reaching a hitch rack and a trail junction—take the left (south) fork and walk a few more steps to the north edge of Fern Lake. A few hundred more feet, following the trail clockwise around the lake to a log bridge, brings you to the best views of the lake and the peaks behind it: Joe Mills Mountain (11,078 feet/3377 m) on the far left; Notchtop Mountain (12,129 feet/3697 m) and Little Matterhorn (11,586 feet/3531 m) on the right. Fern Lake is known to contain greenback and Colorado River cutthroat trout and is open to catch-and-release fishing with barbless hooks only.

When you're ready to head back, retrace your steps to the trailhead.

GOING FARTHER

A side trip to Cub Lake (Hike 8) is possible on your way back and adds several miles to your hike, the total depending on whether you take the Cub Lake Trail back to the Cub Lake Trailhead and walk about 0.8 mile (1.3 km) on the dirt road back to the Fern Lake Trailhead, or hike from the Fern Lake Trail/Cub Lake Trail junction to Cub Lake (1.1 miles/1.8 km from the junction) and return to the junction to finish your hike on the Fern Lake Trail.

10   BIERSTADT LAKE LOOP

Distance: 3.2 miles (5.2 km)
Elevation gain: 675 feet (206 m)
High point: 9455 feet (2882 m)
Difficulty: Medium
Trail surface: Dirt, rock

Maps: USGS McHenrys Peak, USGS Longs Peak, National
Geographic Trails Illustrated Map 200: Rocky Mountain
National Park
GPS: 40.320438°, –105.623687°
Notes: High altitude; be aware of exposure to afternoon
thunderstorms; toilet at trailhead

> Enjoy a walk through the forest encircling a high lake, earned
> by a short but steep hike with views of the peaks of the Con-
> tinental Divide.

GETTING THERE

Driving: From the Estes Park Visitor Center, turn left (west)
onto US Highway 34 (Big Thompson Avenue) and drive 0.2
mile (0.3 km), merging onto US 36 (Elkhorn Avenue) for
0.4 mile (0.6 km). Turn left to stay on US 36 and follow it west
for 3.8 miles (6.1 km) into Rocky Mountain National Park,

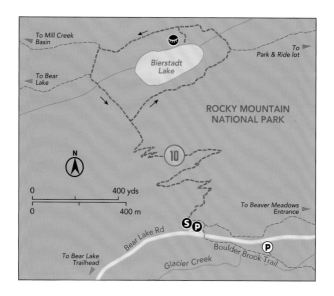

through the Beaver Meadows Entrance Station. About 1000 feet (305 m) past the entrance station, turn left onto Bear Lake Road and follow it for 6.8 miles (10.9 km) to the Bierstadt Lake Trailhead parking lot on the right.

Transit: Drive to the RMNP Park & Ride lot on Bear Lake Road (5.1 miles/8.2 km from US 36; see driving directions above) and take the Bear Lake Route shuttle bus to the Bierstadt Lake Trailhead, about a 5-minute ride from the Park & Ride lot. Or take the Hiker Shuttle Express bus from the Estes Park Visitor Center, then take the Bear Lake Route shuttle bus to the Bierstadt Lake Trailhead.

ON THE TRAIL

If you're on one of the park's Park & Ride buses, you might notice that of all the trailheads, Bierstadt Lake seems to get fewer visitors than its popular neighbors just up the road, Bear Lake and Glacier Gorge. That's not because this is a "boring" hike, at least in some opinions; it just has far less word of mouth, takes a little work to get to the lake (compared to Bear Lake, which is 100 feet/31 m from the parking lot), and doesn't have as many nearby options from the trailhead.

The trail leaves the northwest corner of the parking lot (another trail leaves the northeast corner of the parking lot—you don't want that one) and begins climbing through trees almost right away. About 50 feet (15 m) up the trail, stay left (west) at a trail junction to continue up the rocky trail through trees, which thin out after about 200 vertical feet (61 m). The trail climbs the south edge of the Bierstadt Moraine, made of deposits left over from an ice age glacier—Bierstadt Lake sits on the plateau at the top of the moraine, which is about a mile wide between Glacier Creek (which roughly parallels Bear Lake Road) and Mill Creek (roughly parallel to Glacier Creek, about 1.5 miles/2.4 km north). As you leave the trees, the trail climbs up the sunny hillside through sagebrush and

Bierstadt Lake's north shore offers a fine view of peaks along the Continental Divide.

wildflowers (aster, scarlet paintbrush, mountain harebell, and others), with views to the west of a few of the peaks of the Continental Divide: Thatchtop (12,668 feet/3861 m), Otis Peak (12,486 feet/3806 m), and Hallett Peak (12,713 feet/3875 m). Don't worry, this won't be your last view of the high peaks (and you'll actually get a better view of them at Bierstadt Lake).

At about the 1-mile mark (1.6 km), you reenter dense forest (after your climb up, you might be thankful for the shade), and the trail will flatten out as you reach the southern edge of the Bierstadt Plateau, descending slightly to a trail junction—this is the loop trail around Bierstadt Lake. You can choose to walk either way; for this book, we'll go counterclockwise. At 1.1 miles (1.8 km), the trail passes a hitch rack (for horses) and a social trail heading north to the lake; stay on the main trail heading east. At 1.4 miles (2.3 km), stay on the left (north) at a junction with the trail to the Park & Ride, and at 1.6 miles (2.6 km), reach another junction with a spur trail that heads south about 200 feet (61 m) to the northeast shore of the lake, where you have a great view of not only the tree-ringed Bierstadt Lake, but the skyline of peaks of the Continental Divide, from Longs Peak (14,259 feet/4346 m) on your far left (south) to Flattop Mountain (12,324 feet/3756 m) on your far right (west). When you're done taking photos here, retrace your steps on the spur trail 200 feet (61 m) back to the main trail, and take the left (west) fork.

As you round the lake, you encounter two more trail junctions—stay on the left fork at each of them, continuing south and following the signs for the trail around the lake. At the next junction (2.1 miles/3.4 km)—where the lollipop part of the loop began—take the right fork, following the sign to the Bierstadt Trailhead. Back on the trail you climbed up earlier, continue for 1.1 miles (1.8 km) back your starting point.

11 MORAINE PARK LOOP

Distance: 4.8 miles (8.5 km)
Elevation gain: 100 feet (31 m)
High point: 8092 feet (2466 m)
Difficulty: Medium
Trail surface: Dirt, rock, dirt road, asphalt road
Maps: USGS Longs Peak, National Geographic Trails Illustrated Map 200: Rocky Mountain National Park
GPS: 40.356182°, –105.615773°
Notes: High altitude; be aware of exposure to afternoon thunderstorms; toilet at trailhead; catch-and-keep fishing in the river, streams, and ponds in the Moraine Park

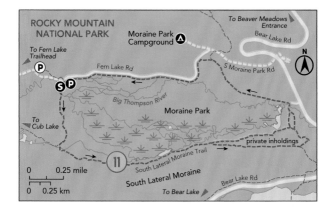

Hike on a mostly flat trail around the perimeter of the glacial Moraine Park, with opportunities to see elk herds in the early fall, as well plenty of places to fish.

GETTING THERE

Driving: From the Estes Park Visitor Center, turn left (west) onto US Highway 34 (Big Thompson Avenue) and drive 0.2 mile (0.3 km), merging onto US 36 (Elkhorn Avenue) for 0.4 mile (0.6 km). Turn left to stay on US 36 and follow it west for 3.8 miles (6.1 km) into Rocky Mountain National Park, through the Beaver Meadows Entrance Station. About 1000 feet (305 m) past the entrance station, turn left onto Bear Lake Road and follow it for 1.3 miles (2.1 km), turning right (southwest) onto Moraine Park Road. Stay on Moraine Park Road for 0.5 mile (0.8 km), turning left (south) onto Fern Lake Road and following it for 1.3 miles (2.1 km) to the Cub Lake Trailhead on the left. If the lot is full, there are a couple of overflow lots about 800 feet (244 m) farther down Fern Lake Road.

Transit: Drive to the RMNP Park & Ride lot on Bear Lake Road (5.1 miles/8.2 km from US 36; see driving directions above) and take the Moraine Park Route shuttle bus to the

Cub Lake Trailhead, about a 20-minute ride from the Park & Ride lot. Or take the Hiker Shuttle Express bus from the Estes Park Visitor Center, then take the Moraine Park Route shuttle bus to the Cub Lake Trailhead.

ON THE TRAIL

The Moraine Park Valley is unique to the hikes on the east side of the park in this book: a leisurely walk around a valley that was once a glacial lake, with almost no elevation gain. It can be tackled in either direction, but for the purposes of this book, we'll go counterclockwise. From the Cub Lake Trailhead, the trail heads south out of the parking lot, almost immediately crossing a wide bridge over the Big Thompson River—at this point, about 10 miles (16.1 km) downstream from its headwaters, it is a quite calm but wide stream. For the next half mile, the trail traces the west edge of the Moraine Park, a marshy area dotted with wildflowers and sagebrush, and in the fall, home to large herds of elk. During the first half of the 1900s, Moraine Park was home to Steads Ranch, a resort that included guesthouses, a hotel, rodeo grounds, and a golf course. In the 1960s, the park purchased the property, removed the buildings, and reseeded the golf course with native grasses. The valley itself is too wet to support trees other than aspens but is thick with willows and grasses. The steep, tree-covered hillside on the south end of the valley is the lateral moraine, made up of debris deposited by the former Thompson Glacier, at one time as tall as the top of the South Lateral Moraine.

At about 0.5 mile (0.8 km), stay left (east) at a trail junction (the right fork leads to Cub Lake) to pick up the South Lateral Moraine Trail, which runs beneath the South Lateral Moraine and traces the south edge of the Moraine Park. At 1.1 miles (1.8 km), the trail splits, the right fork going higher

OPPOSITE: *Looking north from the south edge of the Moraine Park*

and the left fork staying low next to the valley, coming back together in a few hundred feet. At 1.2 miles (1.9 km), the trail splits again, coming back together after a few hundred feet again, and then paralleling a stream. All the way on the north horizon, you are able to see the peaks of the Mummy Range, some of which hold a bit of snow until late summer. The trail continues around the south edge of the valley until 1.8 miles (2.9 km), when it splits into two options: the left (north) fork leads to South Moraine Park Road, a dirt road that stays low and traces around the southeast edge of the valley; and the right (south) fork, which is the continuation of the South Lateral Moraine Trail, climbs about 100 feet (31 m) into the trees, curving around to rejoin the road, adding about 0.3 mile (0.5 km) to the hike. Either option will take you past several buildings; these are privately owned residences that are remnants of the resort that once stood here. (If you take the trail instead of the road, the trail has one junction with another trail; at that junction, take the left/north fork.)

Follow the road (or the trail) as it turns north again. The road and trail rejoin each other a few feet south of where the road crosses the Big Thompson River via a concrete and steel bridge. Cross the bridge and, 20 feet (6 m) past the bridge, pass through a gate (make sure to close the gate behind you) and walk west on the dirt road. The fence is part of the park's elk management strategy, which uses elk exclosures to keep elk from browsing sensitive plant life while allowing other species to pass through under the fences. After 0.2 mile (0.3 km) of walking on the road, pass through another gate (make sure to close the gate) and continue west, remaining on the road. Continue on the road/trail for another 0.4 mile (0.6 km) as it starts to turn northwest and head slightly uphill, to an unmarked fork—take the left fork, heading west for 0.1 mile (160 m) to a crossing with Fern Lake Road. Turn left (south) onto Fern Lake Road and walk the road the final 1.1 miles (1.8 km) back to the Cub Lake Trailhead, being careful of car and bus traffic on the road as you walk.

12 BLACK LAKE

Distance: **9.8 miles (15.8 km)**
Elevation gain: **1480 feet (451 m)**
High point: **10,640 feet (3243 m)**
Difficulty: **Hard**
Trail surface: **Dirt, rock**
Maps: USGS McHenrys Peak, National Geographic Trails Illustrated Map 200: Rocky Mountain National Park
GPS: 40.310567°, −105.640202°
Notes: High altitude; be aware of exposure to afternoon thunderstorms; toilet at trailhead; very limited parking at Glacier Gorge Trailhead; catch-and-keep fishing at Black Lake and Mills Lake

> This stout day hike travels through a glacier-carved gorge, visiting Alberta Falls and three lakes, including Black Lake, surrounded by towering walls on three sides.

GETTING THERE

Driving: From the Estes Park Visitor Center, turn left (west) onto US Highway 34 (Big Thompson Avenue) and drive 0.2 mile (0.3 km), merging onto US 36 (Elkhorn Avenue) for 0.4 mile (0.6 km). Turn left to stay on US 36 and follow it west for 3.8 miles (6.1 km) into Rocky Mountain National Park, through the Beaver Meadows Entrance Station. About 1000 feet (305 m) past the entrance station, turn left onto Bear Lake Road and follow it for 8.3 miles (13.4 km), turning left into the Glacier Gorge Trailhead parking lot.

Transit: Drive to the RMNP Park & Ride lot on Bear Lake Road (5.1 miles/8.2 km from US 36; see driving directions above) and take the Bear Lake Route shuttle bus to the Glacier Gorge Trailhead, about a 10-minute ride from the Park & Ride lot. Or take the Hiker Shuttle Express bus from the Estes Park Visitor Center, then take the Bear Lake Route shuttle bus to the Glacier Gorge Trailhead.

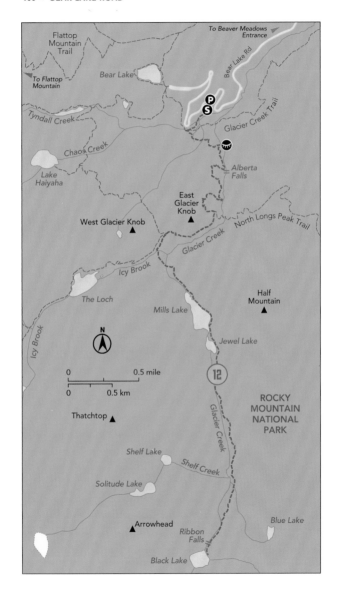

ON THE TRAIL

The hike to Black Lake travels a few miles beyond Alberta Falls (Hike 2) and Mills Lake (Hike 4), but will reward you with views of an alpine lake that you'll share with far fewer people than the first parts of the hike. The trail heads southwest out of the parking lot, then winds through an evergreen forest with a handful of aspens, dotted with large boulders. At the first trail junction, about 0.25 mile (0.4 km) from the trailhead parking lot, stay straight (right). At 0.3 mile (0.5 km), you reach a signed trail junction—head left, following the sign to Alberta Falls.

At 0.6 mile (1 km), you'll be able to hear, and then see from a viewpoint to the left of the trail, the waters of Glacier Creek rushing downhill. The creek roughly parallels nearby Bear Creek Road for a couple of miles before it joins the Big Thompson River just west of Estes Park, then flows through town and into Lake Estes. Alberta Falls is just uphill from you now—follow the trail for another 0.3 mile (0.5 km) to the three-story-high waterfall.

During the busy season, you might not have the waterfall to yourself, but if you scramble around on the rocks a bit, you can usually find a spot to sit and enjoy it. The water rushing down in front of you was very recently snowmelt on the peaks surrounding Glacier Gorge, upstream from Alberta Falls: Longs Peak, Pagoda Mountain, Chiefs Head Peak, McHenrys Peak, and Arrowhead. The water first fills Black Lake below the peaks before traveling downstream to Jewel Lake and Mills Lake, then dropping another few hundred feet to the top of Alberta Falls.

The trail continues a gradual climb through thinning evergreen forest, passing the junction with the North Longs Peak Trail at 1.5 miles (stay south/right). At the 1.6-mile (2.6 km) mark, the trail turns a corner to go south/southwest around the base of East Glacier Knob, one of two lumps of rock that rise about 400 feet (122 m) above the trail at the north end of

Glacier Gorge. The turn in the trail presents an open preview of the alpine scenery you're headed toward. It's also at this point that you'll get an indication of the weather above in Glacier Gorge for the day: if it's going to be cold and windy, you'll get an abrupt blast of air in the face as you turn the corner. Not necessarily a sign you should turn back, but definitely a sign of what the temperature will be like at Mills Lake, a little more than a mile (1.6 km) up the trail and 200 feet (61 m) higher.

At the trail junction at 2 miles (3.2 km), continue left on the Glacier Gorge Trail to Mills Lake—heading straight would take you toward The Loch (Hike 5), a great day hike as well (and a 1.5-mile/2.4 km roundtrip detour on your way back, if you'd like). Just after the trail junction, cross Icy Brook, then Glacier Creek, and a few hundred feet farther, your route skirts the north edge of Mills Lake; take a break and enjoy the view. The 1500-foot-long (457 m) lake, which contains greenback cutthroat trout, brook trout, and rainbow trout, spans the bottom of Glacier Gorge at the base of sweeping walls carpeted with conifers. On the left-hand (east) skyline above the lake, you can see the west face of Longs Peak (14,259 feet/4346 m), and to its right the towers of the Keyboard of the Winds (hopefully you won't have enough wind to find out how they got their name—from the noise they make when high winds rake across them), then the long North Buttress of Pagoda Mountain (13,497 feet/4114 m), Chiefs Head Peak (13,579 feet/4139 m), and just in front of and below Chiefs Head, the pointed Spearhead (12,575 feet/3833 m).

There's a small rock peninsula at the north end of Mills Lake just large enough for four or five people to sit on; if you're lucky enough to find it unoccupied, it makes a great spot for lunch and photos.

OPPOSITE: *Black Lake, with McHenrys Peak behind*

After passing Mills Lake, continue on the Glacier Gorge Trail past Jewel Lake, which is just 0.25 mile (0.4 km) past Mills Lake—you may not notice that it's a separate lake at first. At around the 3.3-mile mark (5.3 km) of your hike, you'll start to encounter some marshy areas, because of the run-off from the mountainside above, most of which have had wooden boardwalks built across them by the National Park Service. Enjoy the dry walking and imagine the hike through the muck that you might have had before the boardwalks were built.

The trail continues to wind through the forest at the bottom of the gorge, offering intermittent, changing views of the peaks above Glacier Gorge (from east to west: Longs Peak, Pagoda Mountain—and if you're up early enough, you might see the north buttress of Pagoda lit by the morning sun—the Spearhead, Chiefs Head Peak, McHenrys Peak, and Arrowhead). Gradually ascend as you walk south on the trail until the last half mile, when you climb the last 300 feet (91 m), passing by the rushing cascades of Glacier Creek as you pop out of the trees. A few dozen rock steps lead to Black Lake (contains brook trout) at 4.8 miles (7.7 km), an icy pool surrounded by walls of rock at the base of high peaks. After you've enjoyed a break, retrace your steps back down the trail to the Glacier Gorge Trailhead.

13 FLATTOP MOUNTAIN AND HALLETT PEAK

Distance: 10 miles (16.1 km)
Elevation gain: 3250 feet (991 m)
High point: 12,713 feet (3875 m)
Difficulty: Hard
Trail surface: Dirt, rock, talus
Maps: USGS McHenrys Peak, National Geographic Trails Illustrated Map 200: Rocky Mountain National Park

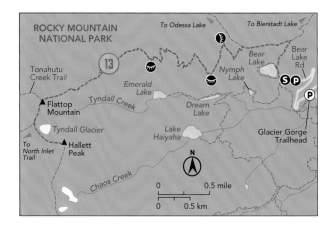

GPS: 40.311869°,–105.645121°

Notes: High altitude; be aware of exposure to afternoon thunderstorms; toilet at trailhead

> This steep hike ends with a short, adventurous scramble to the summit of one of the park's most recognizable peaks, and offers periodic views down to the steep walls of the Tyndall Gorge along the way.

GETTING THERE

Driving: From the Estes Park Visitor Center, turn left (west) onto US Highway 34 (Big Thompson Avenue) and drive 0.2 mile (0.3 km), merging onto US 36 (Elkhorn Avenue) for 0.4 mile (0.6 km). Turn left to stay on US 36 and follow it west for 3.8 miles (6.1 km) into Rocky Mountain National Park, through the Beaver Meadows Entrance Station. About 1000 feet (305 m) past the entrance station, turn left onto Bear Lake Road and follow it for 9.4 miles (15.1 km) to the Bear Lake Trailhead parking lot at the end of the road.

Transit: Drive to the RMNP Park & Ride lot on Bear Lake Road (5.1 miles/8.2 km from US 36; see driving directions above) and take the Bear Lake Route shuttle bus to the Bear

Lake Trailhead, about a 10-minute ride from the Park & Ride lot. Or take the Hiker Shuttle Express bus from the Estes Park Visitor Center, then take the Bear Lake Route shuttle bus to the Bear Lake Trailhead.

ON THE TRAIL

From the Bear Lake Trailhead, walk across the short footbridge next to the ranger cabin and head right, toward Bear Lake. Turn right onto the wide path that circles picturesque Bear Lake, heading counterclockwise around the lake. At the junction at 0.1 mile (160 m), turn right, following the sign to Flattop Mountain. You have more than 3000 feet (914 m) to climb in about 5 miles (8 km) on this hike, and it begins almost immediately with a steady ascent through aspens, pines, and boulders, up and away from the lake. At the 0.4-mile mark (0.6 km), you reach another trail junction—take the left fork following the sign to Flattop Mountain. Your climb continues up a rocky trail with log and stone steps, with views through the trees of Longs Peak, Glacier Gorge, and Otis Peak.

At 0.9 mile (1.5 km), you reach one more trail junction— take the left fork, following the sign to Flattop Mountain, continuing to climb. At 1.3 miles (2.1 km) is a small clearing on the right (south) side at a switchback; it's a nice place to pause for a second and take in the view of the Estes Park valley below. To the far right, not too far in the distance, you can make out a small lake popping up in a sea of evergreen trees—that's Bierstadt Lake (Hike 10).

Continue climbing the rocky trail, coming to the signed Dream Lake Overlook at 1.7 miles (2.7 km), a great place to snap a few photos of Dream Lake, an alpine lake lining the narrow bottom of the gorge below, about 500 feet (152 m) below where you stand. (Dream Lake is one of the four lakes in the Four Lakes Loop, Hike 7.)

OPPOSITE: *A view of Hallett Peak on the hike to Flattop Mountain*

As you continue to ascend, you'll notice that the trees, including Engelmann spruce, and shrubbery grow thinner, and even shorter—by the 2.2-mile mark (3.5 km), the height difference is significant. As you approach tree line, look for flag trees, which are trees with limbs growing primarily (or only) on their leeward side, showing you the direction of prevailing winds.

At 2.5 miles (4 km), looking west, you can just make out Trail Ridge Road, which cuts a thin horizontal strip across the south/southeast side of Sundance Mountain. At 2.8 miles (4.5 km), looking southwest, you'll have a great view of Hallett Peak's northeast-facing wall (the same one you can see from Bear Lake; Hike 1), home to all of its technical rock climbing routes—most of which are 1000 feet (305 m) high or so. A few hundred more feet of walking brings you to tree line, right around 11,300 feet (3444 m).

Just past tree line, pass by the signed Emerald Lake Viewpoint, another great photo spot that looks down on a dark-blue pool surrounded by talus slopes; just past that is a plaque reminding you that the "mountains don't care"—a perfect place to consider how your party is doing and what it will take to get to the top, as you're only about 60 percent there, in terms of mileage and elevation gain.

At 4.4 miles (7.1 km) is the anticlimactic summit of Flattop Mountain: a trail junction sign. There are good views from here, but you definitely won't feel like you're on a summit. For better gratification, and if you're still feeling good, proceed on the unsigned left fork of the trail, heading south and following a cairned route toward Hallett Peak, whose summit should be very visible and obvious to the southeast. The final 200 feet (61 m) to the summit involves some hands-and-feet scrambling up talus and a bit of routefinding (hence the cairns), but isn't too hard—stay toward the right (as opposed to heading left onto the steep north face) and keep going up and you'll find the summit, and great views down into the Tyndall Gorge and Chaos Canyon, as well as over to Longs Peak.

To return to the trailhead, reverse your route, being careful on the downward scramble, and then follow signs back to the Bear Lake Trailhead.

DEVILS GULCH ROAD

The most recognizable feature of the northeast corner of Rocky Mountain National Park is probably the granite domes and slabs of Lumpy Ridge, visible from many points in Estes Park and the namesake of more than one business around town. If you learn the name of only one rock formation during your visit, it will likely be the Twin Owls on Lumpy Ridge. The hikes in this area travel through lower-elevation meadows with numerous patches of wildflowers and views of the formations of Lumpy Ridge and the peaks of the Continental Divide to the south. The exception is Bridal Veil Falls, which leaves from a very small trailhead at the end of a dirt road and travels behind Lumpy Ridge, feeling isolated from the rest of the park.

This corner of the park is less famous than some other areas because it doesn't butt up against the high peaks the park is famous for and thus can be less crowded (although it can be popular during high season). But the hikes in this section, with their views of Lumpy Ridge and the Continental Divide in the distance, can be just as special as the more popular sections of the park, particularly during wildflower season (late June to late August).

OPPOSITE: *The granite formations of Lumpy Ridge as seen from the Black Canyon Trail (Hike 16).*

14 GEM LAKE

Distance: 3.5 miles (5.6 km)

Elevation gain: 1000 feet (305 m)

High point: 8825 feet (2690 m)

Difficulty: Medium

Trail surface: Dirt and rock

Maps: USGS Estes Park, National Geographic Trails Illustrated Map 200: Rocky Mountain National Park

GPS: 40.396543°, –105.512811°

Notes: High altitude; be aware of exposure to afternoon thunderstorms; toilet at trailhead, privy just before the lake

> A short hike with plenty of climbing leads to a small lake nestled between granite walls, in the park's less-visited northeast corner, with views of Estes Park and the Continental Divide on the return trip.

GETTING THERE

From the Estes Park Visitor Center, turn left (west) onto US Highway 34 (Big Thompson Avenue) and drive 0.2 mile (0.3 km). Turn right (north) onto Wonderview Avenue and drive 0.4 mile (0.6 km), turning right (north) onto MacGregor Avenue for 0.8 mile (1.3 km), when MacGregor Avenue curves to the right and becomes Devils Gulch Road. Continue on Devils Gulch Road for 0.6 mile (1 km) and turn left (north) onto Lumpy Ridge Road. Follow Lumpy Ridge Road another 0.3 mile (0.5 km) to the Lumpy Ridge Trailhead parking lot.

ON THE TRAIL

Two trails begin at the Lumpy Ridge Trailhead, and both are just to the west of the restroom—you want the Gem Lake Trail, which splits off and heads to the right (east) behind the restroom. The other trail does loop around Lumpy Ridge eventually and climbs up to Gem Lake from the opposite

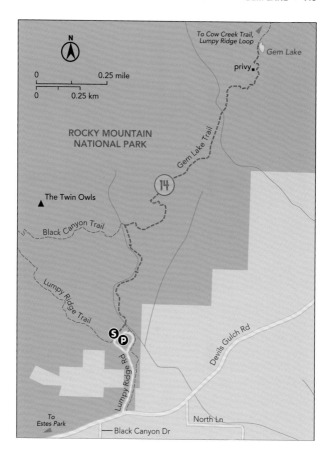

side of the ridge (see Hike 16, Lumpy Ridge Loop), but that's the long way to Gem Lake. This hike is about 8 miles shorter and gets you to the lake much more quickly.

The trail to Gem Lake begins its climb almost immediately out of the parking lot, on dirt and log steps, passing through car-size granite boulders, juniper trees, ponderosa pines, and aspens. At a trail junction at 0.5 mile (0.8 km), take the right (east) fork, following signs to Gem Lake.

Gem Lake from its southeast shore

At about the 0.8-mile (1.3 km) mark, the trees start to open up a bit and you are able to turn around to look back toward the south and have a nice view of Estes Park, as well as the Twin Sisters Peaks to the far left (11,428 feet/3483 m), and the mountains on the Continental Divide, east to west: Mount Meeker (13,911 feet/4240 m), Longs Peak (14,259 feet/4346 m), McHenrys Peak (13,327 feet/4062 m), Powell Peak (13,208 feet/4026 m), and Hallett Peak (12,713 feet/3875 m). You'll definitely notice this view on your way down the trail, but if you look back every once in a while as you hike, you can catch it on your way up too.

At 1.2 miles (1.9 km), cross a log bridge over a creek bed (which is usually dry by midsummer), and then the switchbacks begin to tighten as you climb. At about 1.4 miles (2.3 km), just after you climb a tightly switchbacking set of stone steps is a rock known as "Paul Bunyan's Boot"; it looks like a boot laid down on its heel with a big hole through its sole. If you pass by it without noticing it on your way up, don't fret—it'll be rather obvious on your way back down.

At 1.6 miles (2.6 km), a side trail leads to a privy, a bit of a luxury on a short hiking trail like this. At 1.7 miles (2.7 km), you'll arrive at the south end of Gem Lake and find plenty of spots to sit down for a few minutes. Dragonflies and pesky squirrels will likely be around—don't feed the squirrels, no matter how much they bother you. They're cute, but by feeding them, you're socializing them and encouraging them to rely on handouts from humans, which endangers their survival. And makes them more of a pain for future hikers. To return to the trailhead, reverse your steps, remembering to take a left and head south at the trail junction at about 3 miles (4.8 km) on your way down.

GOING FARTHER

The Lumpy Ridge Loop (Hike 16) continues north of Gem Lake and adds on 7.7 miles (12.4 km) and another 1500 feet (457 m) of elevation gain for a total of 9.4 miles (15 km).

15 BRIDAL VEIL FALLS FROM COW CREEK TRAILHEAD

Distance: 6.2 miles (10 km)
Elevation gain: 990 feet (302 m)
High point: 8789 feet (2679 m)
Difficulty: Medium
Trail surface: Dirt, rock
Maps: USGS Estes Park, National Geographic Trails Illustrated Map 200: Rocky Mountain National Park
GPS: 40.430875°, −105.500543°
Notes: High altitude; be aware of exposure to afternoon thunderstorms; toilet near trailhead; limited parking

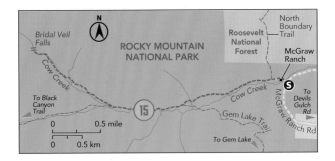

Hike through a historic ranch property and alpine meadows to a 25-foot waterfall in the northeast corner of the park.

GETTING THERE

From the Estes Park Visitor Center, turn left (west) onto US Highway 34 (Big Thompson Avenue) and drive 0.2 mile (0.3 km). Turn right (north) onto Wonderview Avenue and drive 0.4 mile (0.6 km), turning right (north) onto MacGregor Avenue for 0.8 mile (1.3 km), when MacGregor Avenue curves to the right and becomes Devils Gulch Road. Continue on Devils Gulch Road for 2.7 miles (4.4 km), staying left at a Y intersection to turn onto McGraw Ranch Road, and drive 2.2 miles (3.5 km) to the Cow Creek Trailhead parking (parallel parking along the road). Parking is tight (sixteen cars maximum), so an early start is advised.

ON THE TRAIL

The good news is that because of the limited parking, this hike tends to be uncrowded. The bad news is that if you don't get one of the sixteen or so parking spots, you're out of luck that day (unless you have a friend who wants to drop you off and come back in a few hours to pick you up after your hike).

OPPOSITE: *Even in late summer, the 25-foot-high Bridal Veil Falls are worth a visit.*

From the parking area on McGraw Ranch Road, walk north on McGraw Ranch Road to the Y intersection and take the left (west) fork in the road toward the buildings of McGraw Ranch and a gate in the road, where the Cow Creek Trail begins, winding around the backs of the buildings and heading west. This is the old McGraw Ranch, a property with history dating back to 1884 that became part of Rocky Mountain National Park in 1988.

About 1000 feet (305 m) past the gate, near the west edge of McGraw Ranch, is a trail junction with a sign. Stay left (west), following the sign to Bridal Veil Falls. Just after the sign, you pass restrooms on the right (north). The trail remains a two-track road until about 0.6 mile (1 km), when it narrows to single-track and begins a gentle climb up a series of log steps, and then through a meadow dotted with wildflowers. Look for wild bergamot, broadleaf arnica, common yarrow, cutleaf daisies, and others. At the junction at 1.2 miles (1.9 km), stay straight (west), continuing to gradually climb parallel to Cow Creek. Take the right (northwest) fork at the next junction at 2 miles (3.2 km), following the signs to Bridal Veil Falls and passing through another meadow thick with wildflowers. The cap of rock popping out of the trees in the distance above the trail is the summit of Dark Mountain (10,859 feet/3310 m).

In the final mile of trail, climb about 500 vertical feet (152 m) as the trail steepens and gradually enters thicker evergreen trees, crossing Cow Creek twice, and passes through stands of aspen. Around mile 3 (4.8 km), head uphill between two aspens, cross an angling rock slab, and pick up the trail on the other side. The trail switches back twice very quickly and heads left toward the creek again, leading to a set of stone steps. Follow more stone steps and the boulder trail to the base of Bridal Veil Falls, where there are plenty of spots to take photos and many rocks to sit on and take a rest before you turn around and head back the way you came.

GOING FARTHER

Bridal Veil Falls can also be accessed from the Lumpy Ridge Trailhead as an extended side trip of the Lumpy Ridge Loop (Hike 16). This adds 2.2 miles (3.5 km) for a total of 13.4 miles (22 km), or you can opt for a long extension of the Gem Lake Trail (Hike 14) which adds 9.6 miles (15.4 km) for a total of 13.1 miles (21 km).

16 BLACK CANYON TRAIL AND LUMPY RIDGE LOOP

Distance: 8.2 miles (13.2 km)/11.2 miles (18 km)
Elevation gain: 1700 feet (518 m)/2480 feet (756 m)
High point: 9110 feet (2777 m)
Difficulty: Medium/Hard
Trail surface: Dirt, rock
Maps: USGS Estes Park, USGS Glen Haven, National Geographic Trails Illustrated Map 200: Rocky Mountain National Park
GPS: 40.396543°, −105.512811°
Notes: High altitude; be aware of exposure to afternoon thunderstorms; toilet at trailhead, privy on the south side of Gem Lake

> This tour, from below the skyscraper granite slabs and domes of Lumpy Ridge, offers a chance to spot rock climbers and an option to make the hike a longer loop and detour to a high lake.

GETTING THERE

From the Estes Park Visitor Center, turn left (west) onto US Highway 34 (Big Thompson Avenue) and drive 0.2 mile (0.3 km). Turn right (north) onto Wonderview Avenue and drive 0.4 mile (0.6 km), turning right (north) onto MacGregor

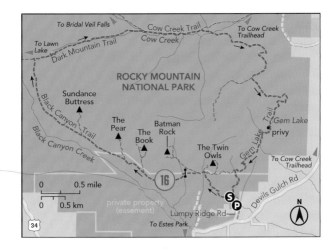

Avenue for 0.8 mile (1.3 km), when MacGregor Avenue curves to the right and becomes Devils Gulch Road. Continue on Devils Gulch Road for 0.6 mile (1 km) and turn left (north) onto Lumpy Ridge Road. Follow Lumpy Ridge Road another 0.3 mile (0.5 km) to the Lumpy Ridge Trailhead parking lot.

ON THE TRAIL

The trail begins at the northwest edge of the parking lot, just west of the restrooms. Two trails split right away near the restroom—you want the one heading west, going through a cattle gate, up a small climb, and then dropping downhill and winding through conifers and aspens. At 0.4 mile (0.6 km), pause for the great view of the Twin Owls, a rock formation locally famous enough to have several businesses named after it. Round a corner for Batman Rock; it's the highest dome on the hillside above the trail. At 0.6 mile (1 km), the trail heads between two large boulders. The opposite side of the boulder on the left (south) features a boulder problem (a short rock-climbing route); if you walk past the boulder and step around to the other side, you may see some climbing chalk. If someone is working the problem, stay off their mat! At 0.7 mile (1.1 km), pass through a cattle gate and into a section of wildflowers: wild bergamot, silvery lupine, cow parsnips, and others. At the trail junction, head left (west), following the sign for Lawn Lake, and at mile 0.8 (1.3 km), you pass a memorial plaque for a climber, and then come to another trail junction—stay left (west) again, following the sign for the Black Canyon Trail. At 1 mile (1.6 km), pass through another cattle gate and enter an easement across private property that enables access to the next section of trail. (Stay on the trail through the section of private property, unless there's a cow on the trail, in which case you should give the animal some space.)

The trail continues at a mellow grade through the meadow below the rock formations, and at mile 1.5 (2.4 km) you start to see some of the formations that are popular with rock climbers: The Book, which has a bunch of parallel vertical cracks on it that look like pages of a book, with the Bookmark Pinnacle just below it and to the left (west). If it's the weekend or any day with sun and warm temperatures, look just to the right (east) of the roof in the rock that looks like the top of a pear, and you might see climbers on a route called *Pear Buttress*, one of the most popular climbs at Lumpy Ridge, and a favorite of local climbing celebrity Tommy Caldwell.

Coming into view at mile 1.8 (2.9 km), the towering Sundance Buttress forms the far west end of Lumpy Ridge, and is home to many longer, tough rock-climbing routes. Around the 2-mile mark (3.2 km), the trail begins a steady, gradual climb as you pass a climbing access trail that heads uphill and north to The Pear. As you continue up the Black Canyon Trail (staying left/northwest), the real quad workout begins: you'll climb almost 1400 feet (427 m) in the next 2 miles

(3.2 km). If you're feeling like a more casual outing today, this is a good spot to turn around and head back to the trailhead, for a 4-mile out-and-back.

If you're in for more of a workout and some climbing through a nice forest, however (or you want to do the entire 11-mile [17.7 km] Lumpy Ridge Loop), keep heading northwest. At mile 2.3 (3.7 km), you pop back into the shade of the ponderosa pines. At mile 2.8 (4.5 km), pass the turnoff for the climbing access trail to Sundance Buttress (stay left/northwest here), and enjoy the ascent through the trees. At 4 miles (6.4 km), you reach the Dark Mountain Trail junction where you have two options: (1) head back the way you came and take in the view of the Lumpy Ridge rock formations from the opposite direction for an 8.2-mile out-and-back, or (2) finish the 11-mile Lumpy Ridge Loop. One reason you should do the Lumpy Ridge Loop, provided you have enough water, snacks, and energy: you've done about 60 percent of the climbing of the Lumpy Ridge Loop already, and the next 2.7 miles (4.4 km) of trail is almost continuous downhill and includes—in season—maybe the densest section of wildflowers of any trail in this book.

If you decide to continue, head right (northeast) at the junction, following the sign to the Cow Creek Trailhead, and enjoy the downhill. At 5.1 miles (8.2 km), take note of the thousands of wildflowers: wild bergamot, scarlet paintbrush, mountain harebell, and others. At 5.6 miles (9 km), pass the turnoff for the Peregrine backcountry campsite (continue right/east), and at 5.7 miles (9.2 km), cross the creek on a log bridge. At the next junction, take the right fork heading southeast, following the sign to the Cow Creek Trailhead. In a few hundred feet, the trail begins to parallel Cow Creek.

At mile 6.4 (10.3 km), stay left (east) as you pass the junction with the trail to the Rabbit Ears backcountry campsite,

OPPOSITE: *Looking southeast along the Black Canyon Trail*

and 0.2 mile (0.3 km) later, at the next junction, turn right (southeast) following the sign to the Lumpy Ridge Trailhead. The trail heads downhill briefly, crossing Cow Creek on a log bridge, and your long downhill stint has finally come to an end as you begin the climb toward Gem Lake, first gradually, and more steeply after about a mile. At 8.2 miles (13.2 km), turn left (southeast), following the signs for Gem Lake and the Lumpy Ridge Trailhead, and enjoy a brief break in the sustained climbing before the final ascent of about 200 vertical feet (61 m) to the lake at mile 9.1 (14.7 km).

At mile 9.4 (15.1 km), you pop out to the welcome oasis of Gem Lake, surrounded by rock walls, with plenty of spots to sit and take a break before you finish the final downhill stretch of trail back to the trailhead. Dragonflies and pesky squirrels will likely be around—don't feed the squirrels, no matter how much they bother you. They're cute, but by feeding them, you're socializing them and teaching them to rely on handouts from humans, which endangers their survival—and makes them more of a pain for future hikers. There's a privy about 1000 feet (305 m) down the trail past the south end of the lake, convenient if you need a restroom stop on your way down.

As you descend, keep an eye out for a rock formation called Paul Bunyan's Boot, which looks like a boot laid down on its heel with a big hole through its sole; it's about a quarter mile down the trail from the south end of Gem Lake. At about mile 10.2 (16.4 km), the trail opens up to a view of Estes Park, as well as the Twin Sisters Peaks to the far left (11,428 feet/3483 m), and the mountains on the Continental Divide, from east to west: Mount Meeker (13,911 feet/4240 m), Longs Peak (14,259 feet/4346 m), McHenrys Peak (13,327 feet/4062 m), Powell Peak (13,208 feet/4026 m), and Hallett Peak (12,713 feet/3875 m).

At the trail junction at mile 10.6 (17.1 km), turn left (south), following the sign to the Lumpy Ridge Trailhead, and stay right at mile 11 (17.7 km) to go through the cattle gate to the trailhead parking lot and your car.

GOING FARTHER

If you're feeling strong and have plenty of water and food, adding a side trip to Bridal Veil Falls from the trail junction at 5.6 miles (9 km) adds 2.2 miles (3.5 km) and about 500 feet (152 m) of elevation gain.

COLORADO HIGHWAY 7

Colorado Highway 7 parallels the park's eastern edge, winding along the border between the Front Range foothills and the mountains, and below the giants of 14,259-foot (4346 m) Longs Peak and 13,911-foot (4240 m) Mount Meeker, the two highest mountains in Rocky Mountain National Park.

Not all the trails along the Highway 7 corridor climb into the high alpine—in fact, this section has a very diverse mix of hikes, from the fully ADA-accessible Lily Lake Trail (Hike 17) to the most difficult hike in this book, the summit route to Longs Peak via the Keyhole Route (Hike 25). The hikes to other peaks in this section—Lily Mountain, Estes Cone, and Twin Sisters Peaks—are much shorter but just as steep, and provide challenging days and unique views of Longs, Meeker, and the other high peaks of the park.

The far southeast corner of the park, the Wild Basin area, also holds some gems. They can feel like well-kept secrets because of their distance from Estes Park, the access at the end of a dirt road, and the small parking lot at the trailhead. For those who make the effort, the rewards include dazzling waterfalls and a greater sense of solitude than is found elsewhere in the park.

OPPOSITE: *The east face of Longs Peak; Chasm Junction is where the trail splits to lead to either Chasm Lake (Hike 24) or Longs Peak via the Keyhole Route (Hike 25).*

17 LILY LAKE

Distance: 1 mile (1.6 km)
Elevation gain: Negligible
High point: 8935 feet (2723 m)
Difficulty: Easy
Trail surface: Packed dirt and gravel, boardwalk
Maps: USGS Longs Peak, National Geographic Trails Illustrated Map 200: Rocky Mountain National Park
GPS: 40.306597°, −105.537685°
Notes: High altitude; be aware of exposure to afternoon thunderstorms; toilet at trailhead; catch-and-release fishing

> A flat, level, fully accessible trail lined with wildflowers loops around a scenic lake with views of Longs Peak and Mount Meeker.

GETTING THERE

From the Estes Park Visitor Center, turn left (west) onto US Highway 34 (Big Thompson Avenue) and drive 0.2 mile (0.3 km). Turn left (southeast) onto Colorado Highway 7 (N. St. Vrain Avenue) and drive south for 0.4 mile (0.6 km), taking a slight right to continue on CO 7. Drive for 6.4 miles (10.3 km) to the Lily Lake Trailhead (parking lots on both sides of the road).

ON THE TRAIL

Lily Lake, added relatively recently (1992) to Rocky Mountain National Park, provides a relaxed walk on a loop trail through a high meadow with a fantastic backdrop. Clockwise or counterclockwise, you'll have views of the two highest peaks in Rocky Mountain National Park, 13,911-foot (4240 m) Mount Meeker and 14,259-foot (4346 m) Longs Peak during the first half or second half of your hike, depending on which

The boardwalk on the south shore of Lily Lake makes for easy hiking.

direction you choose to walk. The trail, packed gravel and dirt with a few sections of flat boardwalk, is fully ADA accessible and stroller-friendly.

This description assumes you've chosen to travel counterclockwise around Lily Lake so the stunning views of big peaks over the lake (and Estes Cone, the shorter, tree-lined peak with a rocky summit in front of Longs and Meeker) will

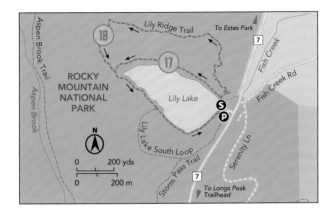

come during the first half of your hike. At the junction at 0.25 mile, where a trail branches off to the right (see Going Farther), stay left to continue around the lake.

As you round the north edge of Lily Lake, you pass underneath a craggy outcrop above the lake and may see rock climbers with backpacks and ropes headed up or down the steep social trail to the climbing area called Jurassic Park a few hundred feet up the slope. Along both sides of the trail are many alpine wildflowers, including yarrow, cow parsnips, and aspen daisies. Catch-and-release fishing is permitted year-round on the south, west, and north shores of Lily Lake (stocked with greenback cutthroat trout) and from July 1 to April 30 on the east shore, extending 20 yards (18 m) into the lake between the southeast and northeast corners.

GOING FARTHER

The Lily Ridge Trail (Hike 18) branches off to the north at 0.25 mile (0.4 km) from the trailhead, climbing 200 feet (61 m) above the lake, and offers great views from a slightly different perspective. After 0.7 mile (1.1 km), the Lily Ridge Trail rejoins the Lily Lake Trail near the northern end of the lake. This route is not ADA accessible.

18 LILY RIDGE TRAIL

Distance: **1.2 miles (1.9 km)**
Elevation gain: **200 feet (61 m)**
High point: **9115 feet (2778 m)**
Difficulty: **Easy**
Trail surface: **Dirt, rock**
Maps: **USGS Longs Peak, National Geographic Trails Illustrated Map 200: Rocky Mountain National Park**
GPS: **40.306597°, −105.537685°**
Notes: **High altitude; be aware of exposure to afternoon thunderstorms; toilet at trailhead**

A side trail off the Lily Lake Trail offers a short climb to views of Lily Lake with Longs Peak, Mount Meeker, and Estes Cone as a backdrop before rejoining the Lily Lake Trail.

GETTING THERE

From the Estes Park Visitor Center, turn left (west) onto US Highway 34 (Big Thompson Avenue) and drive 0.2 mile (0.3 km). Turn left (southeast) onto Colorado Highway 7 (N. St. Vrain Avenue) and drive south for 0.4 mile (0.6 km), taking a slight right to continue on CO 7. Drive for 6.4 miles (10.3 km) to the Lily Lake Trailhead (parking lots on both sides of the road).

ON THE TRAIL

From the Lily Lake Trailhead parking, walk a short distance on the Lily Lake Trail counterclockwise to the junction with the Lily Ridge Trail, which heads northeast and begins switchbacking uphill almost immediately—nearly all of the 200 feet (61 m) of the climbing on this trail is at the beginning (abrupt, but over with quickly). The trail continues to climb through boulders and then to a view of Twin Sisters Peaks back to the east, before turning back west to gradually

From left, Mount Meeker, Longs Peak, and Estes Cone above Lily Lake as viewed from the Lily Ridge Trail

ascend through trees and across a rock slab, continuing on the other side of the slab to a log bench at 0.3 mile. The view from here takes in, from left to right, 13,911-foot (4240 m) Mount Meeker and 14,259-foot (4346 m) Longs Peak, with 11,006-foot (3355 m) Estes Cone, which is all trees on steep slopes until its rocky summit pokes out in the foreground just to the right of Longs Peak.

Traverse across the mountainside on the sandy trail with minor ups and downs before beginning a gradual descent to a series of rock steps that curve down and left at 0.6 mile (1 km). The trail bends back southeast and downhill toward the lake, reaching a trail junction at 0.7 mile (1.1 km). Continue on the left fork (southeast) here to join the Lily Lake Trail at 0.8 mile (1.3 km). Continue counterclockwise around the lake for the full 1.2-mile loop, or clockwise around the lake to head back to the trailhead via the shorter route.

19 COPELAND FALLS

Distance: 1 mile (1.6 km)
Elevation gain: 80 feet (24 m)
High point: 8600 feet (2621 m)
Difficulty: Easy
Trail surface: Dirt, rock
Maps: USGS Allens Park, National Geographic Trails Illustrated Map 200: Rocky Mountain National Park
GPS: 40.208107°, −105.566440°
Notes: High altitude; be aware of exposure to afternoon thunderstorms; toilet at trailhead; small parking lot can fill quickly, especially on summer weekends; catch-and-keep fishing in North St. Vrain Creek

Enjoy an easy walk to a set of peaceful waterfalls in a more remote location outside the main attractions of Rocky Mountain National Park, with options for more challenging hiking beyond the waterfalls.

GETTING THERE

From the Estes Park Visitor Center, turn left (west) onto US Highway 34 (Big Thompson Avenue) and drive 0.2 mile (0.3 km). Turn left (southeast) onto Colorado Highway 7 (N. St. Vrain Avenue) and drive south for 0.4 mile (0.6 km), taking a slight right to continue on CO 7, and drive 12.8 miles (20.6 km), turning right (west) onto County Road 84 at the sign reading "Rocky Mountain National Park Wild Basin." Drive

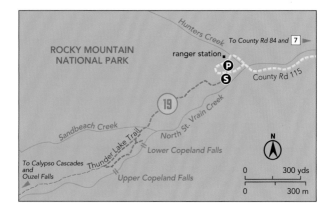

for 0.4 mile (0.6 km), taking a slight right onto County Road 115 (narrow dirt road), and drive 2.2 miles (3.5 km) to the Wild Basin Trailhead parking lot at the end of the road.

ON THE TRAIL

Because of the longer drive from Estes Park and the limited parking at the trailhead, the trails in the Wild Basin section of Rocky Mountain National Park hardly ever feel crowded, even if the parking lot is full. That said, Copeland Falls is the shortest, easiest hike in this part of the park, and several longer hikes use this first section of trail as their start, so if any trail in this area feels popular, it's probably this one. But if you'd like to spend a few minutes taking in the sight and sound of a rumbling cascade of water, it's hard to find a more relaxed approach in the park.

Copeland Falls is a set of two waterfalls: Lower Copeland Falls, in which North St. Vrain Creek plunges about 4 feet (1.2 m), and Upper Copeland Falls, a more drawn-out series of cascades about 500 feet (152 m) upstream from Lower Copeland Falls. To see them both, hike west out of the

OPPOSITE: *Upper Copeland Falls in late summer*

trailhead parking lot on a flat dirt trail through Douglas fir and aspen trees, coming to a turnoff to the left (south) for Lower Copeland Falls at about the 0.3-mile (0.5 km) mark. Follow this to see Lower Copeland Falls, and then continue upstream on the trail next to the creek, which parallels the main trail for a little more than a tenth of a mile to Upper Copeland Falls. You can rejoin the main trail, where the Copeland Falls side trail intersects it near the upper falls, or retrace your steps to return the way you came.

As with most mountain waterfalls, Copeland Falls will be bigger and faster with spring runoff in June and settle down as the snowmelt decreases throughout the summer.

GOING FARTHER
Continue west up the trail to more challenging terrain to Calypso Cascades and Ouzel Falls (Hike 20).

20 THREE WATERFALLS

Distance: 5.4 miles (8.7 km)
Elevation gain: 890 feet (271 m)
High point: 9415 feet (2870 m)
Difficulty: Medium
Trail surface: Dirt, rock
Maps: USGS Allens Park, National Geographic Trails Illustrated Map 200: Rocky Mountain National Park
GPS: 40.208107°, −105.566440°
Notes: High altitude; be aware of exposure to afternoon thunderstorms; toilet at trailhead; catch-and-keep fishing in North St. Vrain Creek

Admire not just one or two, but three distinct waterfalls on a single out-and-back hike, in the park's lesser-visited Wild Basin Area.

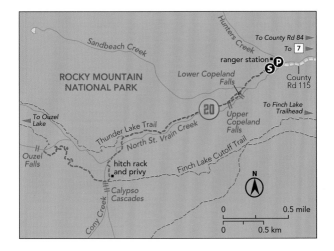

GETTING THERE

From the Estes Park Visitor Center, turn left (west) onto US Highway 34 (Big Thompson Avenue) and drive 0.2 mile (0.3 km). Turn left (southeast) onto Colorado Highway 7 (N. St. Vrain Avenue) and drive south for 0.4 mile (0.6 km), taking a slight right to continue on CO 7, and drive 12.8 miles (20.6 km), turning right (west) onto County Road 84 at the sign reading "Rocky Mountain National Park Wild Basin." Drive for 0.4 mile (0.6 km), taking a slight right onto County Road 115 (narrow dirt road), and drive 2.2 miles (3.5 km) to the Wild Basin Trailhead parking lot at the end of the road.

ON THE TRAIL

The three waterfalls on this trail become increasingly dramatic as you hike, from the fairly peaceful Copeland Falls to the rumbling Calypso Cascades to the final four-story drop of Ouzel Falls that rewards you at the turnaround point.

Hike west out of the trailhead parking lot on a flat dirt trail through Douglas fir and aspen trees. In the first half mile of this hike, before you've even broken a sweat, you'll

encounter Copeland Falls, the lowest of the trailside water-falls of North St. Vrain Creek. Copeland Falls is a set of two waterfalls: Lower Copeland Falls, in which the creek plunges about 4 feet (1.2 m), and Upper Copeland Falls, a more drawn-out series of cascades about 500 feet (152 m) upstream from Lower Copeland Falls. To see them both, take the trail to the left (south) for Lower Copeland Falls at about the 0.3-mile (0.5 km) mark. Check out Lower Copeland Falls, and then continue upstream on the trail next to the creek, which parallels the main trail for a little more than a tenth of a mile (160 m) to Upper Copeland Falls. Rejoin the main trail heading west to continue to Calypso Cascades.

At 1.4 miles (2.3 km), reach a junction with a trail leading right (north) to a set of four backcountry campsites. Con-tinue straight (left) here, following the sign to Ouzel Falls and Calypso Cascades and crossing a bridge over North St. Vrain Creek shortly after. (The creek contains greenback cutthroat trout, brown trout, rainbow trout, and brook trout.) The trail begins to climb more steeply via stone and log steps on the left side of the creek, and at 1.8 miles (2.9 km), pass a trail to a hitch rack and privy on the left (east). Continue north on the main trail for another 150 feet (46 m) to a bridge over the creek, and look upstream at Calypso Cascades, a 200-foot (61 m) waterfall rolling over and through a jumble of large boulders and downed trees.

To reach Ouzel Falls, continue up the trail, crossing a series of streams via rockwork and small bridges at mile 2.2 (3.5 km), then begin a short switchbacking climb that opens up views of surrounding ridges and peaks. At mile 2.7 (4.4 km), reach a hitch rack, and 100 feet (31 m) farther, come upon a bridge over the creek. Just before the creek, a short trail to the left (west) leads to a viewpoint of the actual waterfall. You

OPPOSITE: *Ouzel Falls is the third—and most dramatic—of the water-falls on the Three Waterfalls hike.*

can stick to the main trail for a faster return trip, or take the time—and a few extra steps—for second looks at Calypso Cascades and Copeland Falls.

21 LILY MOUNTAIN

Distance: 4 miles (6.4 km)
Elevation gain: 1200 feet (366 m)
High point: 9786 feet (2983 m)
Difficulty: Medium
Trail surface: Dirt, rock, some scrambling at the top
Maps: USGS Longs Peak, National Geographic Trails Illustrated Map 200: Rocky Mountain National Park
GPS: 40.313696°, −105.535365°
Notes: High altitude; be aware of exposure to afternoon thunderstorms; limited parking at trailhead

> This underrated, stout hike to a summit delivers a big payoff with a 360-degree view at the top.

GETTING THERE

From the Estes Park Visitor Center, turn left (west) onto US Highway 34 (Big Thompson Avenue) and drive 0.2 mile (0.3 km). Turn left (southeast) onto Colorado Highway 7 (N. St. Vrain Avenue) and drive south for 0.4 mile (0.6 km), taking a slight right to continue on CO 7, and drive 5.9 miles (9.5 km) to the Lily Mountain Trailhead, a dirt pull-off on the right (west) side of CO 7. The pull-off is big enough for six to eight cars maximum, so if it's full, you may have to find an alternate parking spot along the road before or after the trailhead.

ON THE TRAIL

A little secret about this hike: It's not actually in Rocky Mountain National Park. It's perched right on the park's eastern

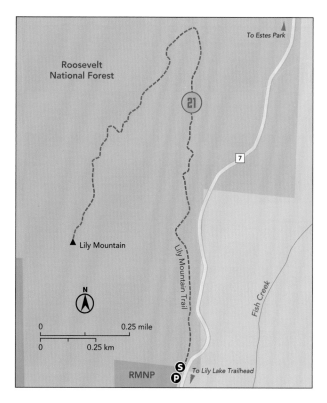

border, but the trailhead, trail, summit, and almost all of Lily Mountain are in Roosevelt National Forest. What does that mean for you? Other than the fact that you can bring your dog on the trail (unlike trails in Rocky Mountain National Park), not much. It's just too good of a hike to leave out of this book on a minor technicality.

The wide, sandy trail is mellow for the first quarter mile through a forest of ponderosa pines, aspens, and Douglas firs. It then begins climbing a set of stone steps and rolls up and down a bit. At 0.4 mile (0.6 km), the trail appears to fork—stay on the left (west) fork, because the right fork dead-ends in a gully. Cross a gully and return to the well-defined trail on the opposite side of the gully. A brief climb up rock steps and a couple of switchbacks begins at 0.7 mile (1.1 km), then the trail levels out again. At 0.8 mile (1.3 km), you see a large fin of rock abutting the trail on the (right) east side. The side of the rock facing away from the trail has been

developed as a rock-climbing area. You may see (or hear) some rock climbers here, and even if no one's climbing, you can walk around to the side opposite the trail and try to spot some of the bolts leading up the rock face in several spots.

If you like to get all the serious uphill hiking done all at once, you're in luck: at the 1.1-mile mark (1.8 km), the trail begins to climb steeply, 870 feet (265 m) in the next mile. As you walk up the stone and log steps, you can see Rams Horn Mountain (9553 feet/2912 m) through the trees to the west. At 1.9 miles (3.1 km), the trees open for a view of Twin Sisters Peaks (11,428 feet/3483 m) to the east, and then the trail peters out at a large tree fallen down the slope—look up and to your right (west) for a cairn and a sign that says "Trail" mounted on the tree behind it (the sign is very hard to see). Follow the sign, and several cairns, to the summit. Some hands-and-feet scrambling is required in the last 100 feet (31 m) to the summit.

At the top, your efforts are rewarded with a unique experience that most visitors to Rocky Mountain National Park miss: a 360-degree view that includes Twin Sisters Peaks (11,428 feet/3483 m), Mount Meeker (13,911 feet/4240 m), Longs Peak (14,259 feet/4346 m), Estes Cone (11,006 feet/3355 m), Hallett Peak (12,713 feet/3875 m), Ypsilon Mountain (13,514 feet/4119 m), and the granite faces and domes of Lumpy Ridge to the north, as well as the Stanley Hotel (the huge white building with red roof at the northeast edge of Estes Park) and Lake Estes. Looking northwest toward the park and Trail Ridge Road, the brown-roofed buildings in the valley below are the YMCA of the Rockies. Have a seat on a rock and enjoy the view, and retrace your steps down to the trailhead when you're ready.

OPPOSITE: *The peaks of the Continental Divide as you look west from the summit of Lily Mountain*

22 ESTES CONE VIA LONGS PEAK TRAILHEAD

Distance: 6.6 miles (10.6 km)

Elevation gain: 1600 feet (488 m)

High point: 11,006 feet (3355 feet)

Difficulty: Medium

Trail surface: Dirt, rock, talus

Maps: USGS Longs Peak, National Geographic Trails Illustrated Map 200: Rocky Mountain National Park

GPS: 40.271768°, –105.556496°

Notes: High altitude; be aware of exposure to afternoon thunderstorms; toilet at trailhead

> This stout and uncrowded hike features the ruins of an early-twentieth-century mine and a short scramble to a summit with great views of Mount Meeker and Longs Peak.

GETTING THERE

From the Estes Park Visitor Center, turn left (west) onto US Highway 34 (Big Thompson Avenue) and drive 0.2 mile (0.3 km). Turn left (southeast) onto Colorado Highway 7 (N. St. Vrain Avenue) and drive south for 0.4 mile (0.6 km), taking a slight right to continue on CO 7, and drive 9 miles (14.5 km), turning right (west) onto Longs Peak Road at the sign for Longs Peak Area. Drive 1.1 miles (1.8 km) west on Longs Peak Road to the Longs Peak Trailhead.

ON THE TRAIL

There are many ways to take in a view of Longs Peak (14,259 feet/4346 m) and Mount Meeker (13,911 feet/4240 m), the easiest of which doesn't even involve leaving the comfortable front seat of your car. But the top of Estes Cone is one of my favorite spots to sit and enjoy the view of the two peaks because the vantage point shows how rugged both peaks

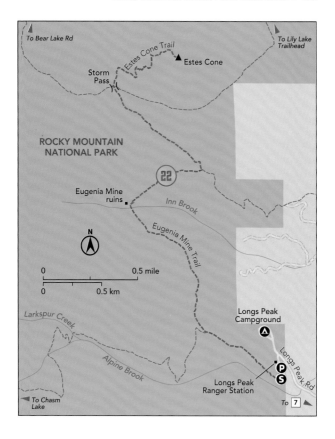

are, and it's also the opposite of sitting in your car: hard to earn. It takes 1600 feet (488 m) of climbing to get to the summit of Estes Cone, and 1300 feet (396 m) of that come in the last 1.4 miles (2.3 km), winding up a rocky path with lots of tree roots poking out, making you work just a little bit harder to achieve uphill progress. But it's worth it to take in the view from the summit.

The Longs Peak Trail heads west and south out of the parking lot before turning to head northwest, climbing through

The view of Mount Meeker and Longs Peak greets you on the summit of Estes Cone.

the trees from the very beginning, coming to a trail junction at 0.5 mile (0.8 km). At the junction, take the right (north) fork, following the sign toward Estes Cone. The trail settles in to a more gradual climb with a lot of roots and rocks. Around 0.6 mile (1 km), you can see the rocky top of Estes Cone straight ahead (north) rising above the trail. The trail heads downhill for a short bit before a steep, rocky climb.

At 1.3 miles (2.1 km), cross a shallow stream on rocks, and then cross two consecutive log bridges as you pass by the Eugenia Mine on the left (west). The remains of the house you see belonged to Carl Norwell, his wife, and two daughters; they even had a piano hauled in by wagon when they lived here. Beginning in 1905, Carl Norwell worked the mine.

A tunnel was dug, purportedly 1000 feet (305 m) deep, and carts sent into it on a track, in the hopes of finding gold. As the sign here says, the mine "produced more dreams than gold," and Norwell abandoned the mine in 1919.

After the mine, the trail continues downhill, past a junction on the right (east) with the trail to the Moore Park backcountry campsites at mile 1.6 (2.6 km), and through a meadow full of wildflowers: scarlet paintbrush, lupine, sulphur flowers, and others. At the trail junction at mile 1.8 (2.9 km), take the left (northwest) fork, following the sign to Estes Cone. Over the next quarter mile, the trees begin to thin as the trail traverses a slope, and then the steep climb begins, up loose rock, log steps, and tree roots. At mile 2.5 (4 km), the trail reaches a four-way intersection at Storm Pass at 10,255 feet (3126 m). At the intersection, continue straight (north), and take your time—you still have 750 feet (229 m) to go up.

The trail can become indistinct in areas after this point— watch for cairns and pay attention to the deadfall that's been laid parallel to the trail in many spots (if you find yourself stepping over a long-dead tree, check yourself and make sure you're still on the trail). At mile 3.2 (4.8 km), follow cairns through a talus field along the base of the rocky crown of the peak. About 30 vertical feet (9 m) of easy scrambling leads to a great viewpoint, a 180-degree view of Longs Peak and Mount Meeker to the southwest, and all the way to the Mummy Range to the northwest. If you want to continue to the proper 11,006-foot (3355-meter) summit, look due east about 60 feet (18 m)—it's an easy walk in that direction, and a short scramble up the south side of the summit block. From there, take in views of the other side—Twin Sisters Peaks (11,428 feet/3483 m) to the east and Lily Lake below to the northeast.

To head back to the trailhead, reverse your steps, taking care both on the scramble down and to not lose the rough trail in the first mile or so off the summit.

23 TWIN SISTERS PEAKS

Distance: 7.2 miles (11.6 km)
Elevation gain: 2350 feet (716 m)
High point: 11,428 feet (3483 m)
Difficulty: Hard
Trail surface: Dirt, rock, talus
Maps: USGS Longs Peak, National Geographic Trails Illustrated Map 200: Rocky Mountain National Park
GPS: 40.303014°, −105.536722°
Notes: High altitude; be aware of exposure to afternoon thunderstorms

> A relentlessly steep climb leads to a summit with 360-degree views of the high peaks of Rocky Mountain National Park, and the foothills and plains to the east.

GETTING THERE

From the Estes Park Visitor Center, turn left (west) onto US Highway 34 (Big Thompson Avenue) and drive 0.2 mile (0.3 km). Turn left (southeast) onto Colorado Highway 7 (N. St. Vrain Avenue) and drive south for 0.4 mile (0.6 km), taking a slight right to continue on CO 7, and drive 6.4 miles (10.3 km). Turn left onto Serenity Lane and drive up the road to a gate. Parallel park on the right side of the road only, before the gate. If parking is full or closed (in spring, winter, and fall), park at the Lily Lake Trailhead (toilet available) and walk on Serenity Lane (on the east side of CO 7) to the trailhead, adding about 0.8 mile (1.2 km) of walking and 180 feet (55 m) of elevation gain to the trip.

ON THE TRAIL

From the gate on Serenity Lane, walk up the road 0.1 mile (160 m) to a small wooden footbridge on the left that leads to a trailhead kiosk. The rocky trail begins climbing here.

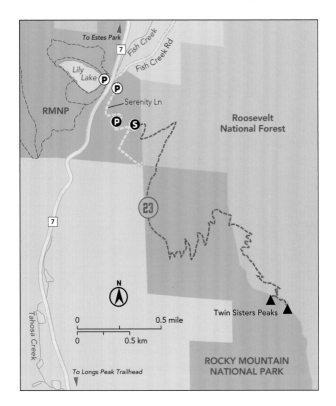

Keep in mind that you've got 2350 feet/716 m to climb in 3.6 miles/5.8 km—there aren't many long flat spots on this trail.

With an early start, you will be in the shade for much of the hike up. The trail climbs steadily up rocks and rock steps and log steps through dense evergreen forest dotted with a few aspens. At the 1-mile mark (1.6 km), you have intermittent views of the rocky cap of Estes Cone through the trees to the west—for reference, the summit of Estes Cone is about 200 feet (61 m) shorter than the summit of Twin Sisters, where you're headed. At mile 1.1 (1.8 km), you see Longs Peak and Mount Meeker to the west through a gap in the trees,

Colorado Highway 7 is far below as you look southwest from the west summit of Twin Sisters Peaks.

and at 1.3 miles (2.1 km), cross a landslide that took out a huge swath of trees above and below the trail after heavy rains in September 2013. The trail steepens after crossing the slide, climbing in increasingly tightening switchbacks for almost a half mile (0.8 km) before relenting.

At mile 2.4 (3.9 km), pass a sign that says "Entering Forest Service Lands." You soon cross over onto the east side of the peak, and, most likely, into the sun for a bit. You go back into Rocky Mountain National Park just before the summit, but this stretch of trail is on Roosevelt National Forest land. Around this point, you start seeing gnarled and hardy limber pines and bristlecone pines, as well as a view to the northwest of high peaks in the park like Ypsilon Mountain (13,514 feet/4119 m). At 2.9 miles (4.7 km), you are above tree line and able to see the twin summits of Twin Sisters. The trail winds through talus to the saddle between the two summits at mile 3.3 (5.3 km), home to a radio antenna and building. Cairned switchbacks north of the building lead to the west summit, where the best photo opportunities lie.

If you want to touch the true summit of Twin Sisters, however, you'll need to return to the saddle and find a faint unmarked trail to the east summit—if you're comfortable with some scrambling near the top of the 70-foot (21 m) climb, you can find your own route to the top, where there's a USGS benchmark. The east summit is 25 feet (7.6 m) higher than the west summit on USGS maps, but you might think they look much closer in height than that.

To return to the trailhead, reverse your steps.

24 CHASM LAKE

Distance: 8.6 miles (13.8 km)
Elevation gain: 2500 feet (762 m)
High point: 11,800 feet (3597 m)
Difficulty: Hard
Trail surface: Dirt, rock, talus
Maps: USGS Longs Peak, National Geographic Trails Illustrated Map 200: Rocky Mountain National Park
GPS: 40.271768°, −105.556496°
Notes: High altitude; be aware of exposure to afternoon thunderstorms; toilet at trailhead; one toilet is available on the trail at Chasm Junction (3.5 miles); bring your own toilet paper; catch-and-keep fishing

A stout day hike above tree line leads to an alpine lake surrounded on three sides by towering walls, including the Diamond of Longs Peak.

GETTING THERE

From the Estes Park Visitor Center, turn left (west) onto US Highway 34 (Big Thompson Avenue) and drive 0.2 mile (0.3 km). Turn left (southeast) onto Colorado Highway 7 (N. St. Vrain Avenue) and drive south for 0.4 mile (0.6 km), taking a slight right to continue on CO 7, and drive 9 miles (14.5 km), turning right (west) onto Longs Peak Road at the sign for Longs Peak Area. Drive 1.1 miles (1.8 km) west on Longs Peak Road to the Longs Peak Trailhead.

ON THE TRAIL

The trail leads west out of the Longs Peak Trailhead parking lot and begins climbing immediately through conifers. At the trail junction at 0.5 mile (0.8 km), stay left (west), following

Sunrise on an early-morning hike to Chasm Lake

the signs to Chasm Lake and Longs Peak. The trail continues to climb through the forest, roughly paralleling Alpine
Brook, the creek you can hear and occasionally see on the
left (south). At the junction with the trail to the Goblins Forest
campsite at 1.2 miles (1.9 km), stay right (west). At 1.6 miles
(2.6 km), the trail crosses Larkspur Creek on a single-log footbridge and, after 0.3 mile (0.5 km) of switchbacks, crosses a
waterfall on a wide log bridge.

At about 2.3 miles (3.7 km), as the trail begins to climb
above tree line, you have your first views of the east-facing
Diamond of Longs Peak, and if you've started hiking early
enough, the face will be glowing pink with the first rays of
sunrise. At the junction with the trail to the Battle Mountain

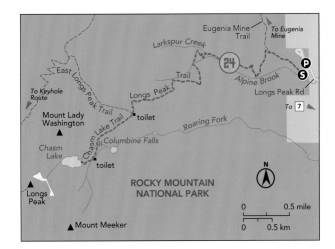

backcountry campsites at 2.8 miles (4.5 km), stay left (south), following the sign to Chasm Lake and Longs Peak as the trail becomes increasingly rocky while switchbacking up the slope.

At 3.5 miles (5.6 km), the trail reaches Chasm Junction, a four-way intersection. To continue, head straight through the intersection on the southwest trail, following the sign to Chasm Lake, but if you'd like to stop and use the toilet, take the far-left (east) trail 150 feet (46 m) to the toilet. The toilet structure here, and the toilets at the Boulderfield, both built by University of Colorado at Denver students to withstand winds of up to 225 mph (362 kmph) and to cut down on waste packed down the mountain by up to 80 percent, won an American Institute of Architects award in 2019.

From Chasm Junction, head southwest on the trail as it traverses the south slope of Mount Lady Washington (13,281 feet/4048 m), passing Columbine Falls above Peacock Pool. At about 3.9 miles (6.3 km), the trail enters Chasm Meadow, crosses a couple of streams via rocks, and passes a spur trail leading east to another award-winning toilet. The trail becomes faint and scrambles up rock just past the Chasm

Lake sign—look for a series of cairns just up and to the right of the sign to find the route. The trail is somewhat indistinct as it climbs steeply; generally stay high and right below a rock wall and step on rocks (stay off the fragile tundra grasses lower and right). A brief scramble through some boulders leads you to the east shore of Chasm Lake and the rock wall cirque behind it, including the nearly 1000-foot-tall (305-m-tall) Diamond. Depending on the season, you may even see climbers on the Diamond or elsewhere on the rock formations surrounding the lake. Take a seat and enjoy the view before heading back down the way you came.

25 LONGS PEAK VIA KEYHOLE ROUTE

Distance: 14.8 miles (23.8 km)
Elevation gain: 4855 feet (1480 m)
High point: 14,259 feet (4346 m)
Difficulty: Hard
Trail surface: Dirt, rock, talus, slabs
Maps: USGS Longs Peak, National Geographic Trails Illustrated Map 200: Rocky Mountain National Park
GPS: 40.271768°, –105.556496°
Notes: High altitude; be aware of exposure to afternoon thunderstorms; toilet at trailhead; two toilets on trail; bring your own toilet paper

This long, high-altitude hike requires commitment and some scrambling to reach the 14,259-foot (4346-m) summit of Longs Peak, the monarch of the Front Range and one of Colorado's most famous mountains.

GETTING THERE
From the Estes Park Visitor Center, turn left (west) onto US Highway 34 (Big Thompson Avenue) and drive 0.2 mile

(0.3 km). Turn left (southeast) onto Colorado Highway 7 (N. St. Vrain Avenue) and drive south for 0.4 mile (0.6 km), taking a slight right to continue on CO 7, and drive 9 miles (14.5 km), turning right (west) onto Longs Peak Road at the sign for Longs Peak Area. Drive 1.1 miles (1.8 km) west on Longs Peak Road to the Longs Peak Trailhead.

ON THE TRAIL

This hike is the PhD of day hiking in Rocky Mountain National Park; it's more difficult than any other hike in this book and should be approached with respect and caution. The Keyhole Route on Longs Peak is only snow- and ice-free for a couple of months in late summer and early fall each year, and sometimes only a few weeks. Conditions are posted on the park's website when the Keyhole Route becomes "nontechnical"—that is, when you can climb it without crampons. Even when the route is rated nontechnical, the mountain is challenging and dangerous because of exposure to weather and steep drop-offs. An early start is mandatory (most hikers start at 2:00 or 3:00 AM) to avoid exposure to afternoon thunderstorms; check weather forecasts and plan on being on your way down from the summit by noon at the latest, and budget more time than you think you need. The upper section of the route can become crowded and because of the number of people (not to mention the thin air at high altitude), it can be slow going. It's a good rule of thumb that the Keyhole, at 6.3 miles (10.1 km), is only halfway (despite the fact that when you get there, you'll have only a little more than 1000 vertical feet/305 m and 1.1 miles/1.8 km to the summit). All that said, plenty of people make it to the summit every year. Many make it partway, turn around, and save the summit for another day, and that's always a prudent bet.

The trail leads west out of the Longs Peak Trailhead parking lot and begins climbing immediately through conifers. At

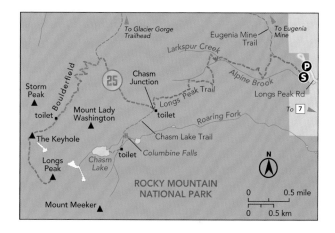

the trail junction at 0.5 mile (0.8 km), stay left (west), following the signs to Chasm Lake and Longs Peak. The trail continues to climb through the forest, roughly paralleling Alpine Brook, the creek you can hear and occasionally see on the left (south). At the junction with the trail to the Goblins Forest campsite at 1.2 miles (1.9 km), stay right (west). At 1.6 miles (2.6 km), the trail crosses Larkspur Creek on a single-log footbridge and, after 0.3 mile (0.5 km) of switchbacks, crosses a waterfall on a wide log bridge.

At about 2.3 miles (3.7 km), as the trail begins to climb above tree line, you have your first views of the east-facing Diamond of Longs Peak, and if you're hiking at sunrise, the face will be glowing pink with the first rays of sun. At the junction with the trail to the Battle Mountain backcountry campsites at 2.8 miles (4.5 km), stay left (south), following the sign to Chasm Lake and Longs Peak as the trail becomes increasingly rocky while switchbacking up the slope.

At 3.5 miles (5.6 km), the trail reaches Chasm Junction, a four-way intersection. To continue up Longs Peak, take the far-right (northwest) trail, following the sign to the Boulderfield, but if you'd like to stop and use the toilet, take the far-left (east) trail 150 feet (46 m) to the toilet. The toilet structure here, and the toilets at the Boulderfield, both built by University of Colorado at Denver students to withstand winds of up to 225 mph (362 kmph) and to cut down on waste packed down the mountain by up to 80 percent, won an American Institute of Architects award in 2019.

Past Chasm Junction, you'll get a short break from switchbacks as you traverse the east slopes of Mount Lady Washington. At the trail junction at 4.4 miles (7.1 km), take the left (southwest) fork, following signs for Longs Peak and the Boulderfield. In the next section of trail, the top of Storm Peak (13,326 feet/4062 m) rises above (Longs Peak's neighbor to the north). At about the 5.2-mile mark (8.4 km), you can just see the Keyhole, just to the left (south) of the low point of the ridge between Longs and Storm Peaks. In the next quarter mile or so (about 0.4 km), the trail can become somewhat indistinct as it winds through tundra grass and boulders—follow cairns to make sure you're on the route, and if you're stepping on plants, you are off the route. Around 5.9 miles (9.5 km), the trail enters the Boulderfield— you may see some tents of people who have camped here the night before and may be climbing Longs today (getting an almost 6-mile/9.7-km head start!), as well as more of those award-winning toilets. Once through the Boulderfield, the route goes through larger boulders up to the Keyhole— don't worry about following every single step of the route through here; just follow cairns and take the line of least resistance, aiming for the Keyhole.

At 6.3 miles (10.1 km), you'll be at the Keyhole and the Agnes Vaille Shelter standing just to the south of it. The shelter was built in 1927 and named for Agnes Vaille, who

OPPOSITE: *Looking down into Glacier Gorge from near the top of The Trough on the Keyhole Route to the top of Longs Peak*

died descending from the first winter ascent of Longs Peak in January 1925. It's not a bad place to have a seat and put on a layer before you head through the Keyhole to finish your climb.

Once through the Keyhole, look left (south) to find the first of many red-and-yellow bull's-eyes painted on rocks to mark the Keyhole Route. Follow these, and if you get to a point where you can't see the next bull's-eye, go back to the previous one and keep looking. It's easy to get off-route during the rest of the climb, but following the bull's-eyes will keep you on the correct route. After the Keyhole, the route is almost completely scrambling around and over boulders, and flat spots to stand are uncommon. No matter how fast you've gone up until this point, the section from the Keyhole

to the summit slows you down because of the terrain and because of the altitude.

From the Keyhole, the route traverses across and up the west face of Longs Peak to the base of the Trough, at roughly mile 6.7 (10.8 km). The Trough is as romantic as it sounds: a long gully filled with boulders and talus, which the bull's-eye route climbs via switchbacks. In the Trough, be careful to not dislodge rocks of any size—you're likely to have climbers below you, and a kicked rock can roll downhill, gain speed, and fly into someone. At the top of the Trough, a few thoughtful scrambling moves will lead you to the Narrows, a short and sometimes exposed section of walking and scrambling along a ledge.

Once through the Narrows, you pop out at the base of the Homestretch, a section of low-angled slabs and cracks that is, believe it or not, the least technical route to the summit. Take your time, nonetheless, and be careful through this section, the final 300 vertical feet (91 m), to reach the wide, flat rocky summit of Longs Peak, the high point of Rocky Mountain National Park at 14,259 feet (4346 m). Take a break, put on a layer, have a snack and some water, and snap some photos before taking a minute to remind yourself that you made it to the summit, but the summit is only halfway to getting home safely, before you head back down the way you came.

OPPOSITE: *Bull's-eyes mark the route.*

TRAIL RIDGE ROAD

Trail Ridge Road, climbing higher than 12,000 feet (3658 m), allows you to experience alpine tundra through your car's windshield. But why limit yourself to that view? Bisecting the park from east to west, the road provides access to a fantastic set of trailheads—trailheads that are the gateway to close-up exploration of that alpine tundra and expansive views of the park's high mountains. And since the road itself is at such a high elevation, you feel like you're already in the middle of the sky before even taking your first step. (Just make sure you're properly acclimated before tackling these hikes!)

Trails ranging from 1 mile to 4 miles (1.6 km to 6.5 km) in length traverse into the tundra, allowing you to experience the harsh but beautiful environment that marmots, pika, and dozens of tough plants call home. The Tundra Communities Trail and the Alpine Ridge Trail provide short, educational jaunts on well-built paths that make it easy to see them for yourself. If you need to limit your time and activity in the area, several of the shorter trails in this section can complement a scenic drive along Trail Ridge Road.

OPPOSITE: *A view west toward Trail Ridge Road from the Deer Mountain Trail (Hike 29)*

26 ALPINE RIDGE TRAIL

Distance: 0.6 mile (1 km)
Elevation gain: 209 feet (64 m)
High point: 12,005 feet (3659 m)
Difficulty: Easy
Trail surface: Stone stairs
Maps: USGS Fall River Pass, USGS Trail Ridge, National
Geographic Trails Illustrated Map 200: Rocky Mountain
National Park
GPS: 40.441539°, −105.753989°
Notes: High altitude; be aware of exposure to afternoon
thunderstorms; toilet, restaurant, and gift shop at trailhead

Get a taste of hiking in thin air via a short but strenuous hike
up stone stairs through alpine tundra to the 12,005-foot high
point nicknamed "Huffers Hill," with expansive views of the
surrounding mountains.

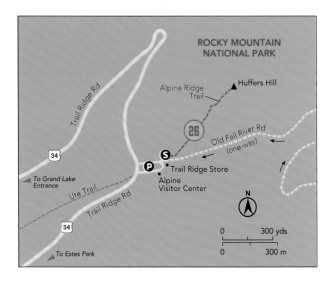

GETTING THERE

From the Estes Park Visitor Center, turn left (west) onto US Highway 34 (Big Thompson Avenue) and drive 0.2 mile (0.3 km), merging onto US 36 (Elkhorn Avenue) for 0.4 mile (0.6 km). Turn left to stay on US 36 and follow it west for 3.8 miles (6.1 km) into Rocky Mountain National Park, through the Beaver Meadows Entrance Station. After the entrance station, continue 2.9 miles (4.2 km) on US 36 to Deer Ridge Junction, and continue straight (the left fork), now on Trail Ridge Road. From the junction, drive another 17 miles (27.4 km), turning right (north) into the Alpine Visitor Center parking lot.

ON THE TRAIL

The Alpine Ridge Trail begins at the east end of the parking lot. The route climbs a set of stairs to a point 12,005 feet (3659 m) above sea level—but you climbed the first 11,796 feet (3595 m) in your car, and the hike is only 0.3 mile (0.5 km) long, so how hard could it be? Answer: Plenty. On a low-traffic day, the drive from Estes Park to the Alpine Visitor Center can take less than an hour, which is great, but it doesn't exactly get your body ready to walk up 220-plus stairs in the thin air. Better to check your ego before you start hiking, take your time, and take breaks when you need to so you can safely get to the top—medical rescues for people experiencing dizziness, chest pains, and shortness of breath do happen on this very short trail. Also: bring a jacket or other layer with you if it's anything but still, warm, and sunny in the parking lot. The entire trail is completely exposed, and even in the middle of summer, a breeze at 12,000 feet (3658 m) can be very chilling. You'll have a much better time if you have a jacket with you and are able to enjoy the view at the top than if you have to rush down because you're shivering in the cold.

The Alpine Ridge Trail is literally a brief bit of asphalt plus a set of stairs, built from 2010 to 2013 to accommodate

The sign at the top of the Alpine Ridge Trail

the traffic of all the folks who wanted to get just a little bit higher than the Alpine Visitor Center. The tundra this high is very fragile and prone to erosion, so the park constructed a durable staircase to the viewpoint in order to preserve the surrounding terrain. Although it can be tempting to step off the stairs to take a photo or rest as you climb the stairs to the top, don't do it—just a few human footfalls in one day can be fatal to the tundra plants at this altitude. Hence the stairs, and the ropes alongside the stairs. Along the trail, you'll see plenty of alpine wildflowers, including yellow stonecrop, goldenweed, pinnate-leaf daisies, and others.

Once you reach the top, enjoy views of the Never Summer Mountains, which run north to south just past the park's western border, and the high peaks directly to the east of the Alpine Visitor Center: from north to south, 13,514-foot (4119 m) Ypsilon Mountain; 13,069-foot (3983 m) Mount Chiquita; and 12,454-foot (3795 m) Mount Chapin. After you're done enjoying the view, retrace your steps back to the trailhead.

27 TUNDRA COMMUNITIES TRAIL

Distance: 1 mile (1.6 km)
Elevation gain: 175 feet (53 m)
High point: 12,285 feet (3745 m)
Difficulty: Easy
Trail surface: Asphalt, stone steps, optional scramble
Maps: USGS Trail Ridge, National Geographic Trails Illustrated Map 200: Rocky Mountain National Park
GPS: 40.412539°, –105.733376°
Notes: High altitude; be aware of exposure to afternoon thunderstorms; toilet at trailhead

> This trail just off Trail Ridge Road feels like a sidewalk across the sky. It makes for a low-commitment, family-friendly way to explore the alpine tundra ecosystem and take in 360-degree views from a high point.

GETTING THERE

From the Estes Park Visitor Center, turn left (west) onto US Highway 34 (Big Thompson Avenue) and drive 0.2 mile (0.3 km), merging onto US 36 (Elkhorn Avenue) for 0.4 mile (0.6 km). Turn left to stay on US 36 and follow it west for 3.8 miles (6.1 km) into Rocky Mountain National Park, through the Beaver Meadows Entrance Station. After the entrance station, continue 2.9 miles (4.7 km) on US 36 to Deer Ridge Junction, and continue straight (the left fork), now on Trail Ridge Road. From the junction, drive another 13 miles (20.9 km), turning right (north) into the Tundra Communities Trail parking lot.

ON THE TRAIL

The trail begins on both the north and south sides of the restroom—crushed rock and stairs on the north side of the restroom, asphalt on the south side of the restroom. The two trails join together after about 50 feet (15 m).

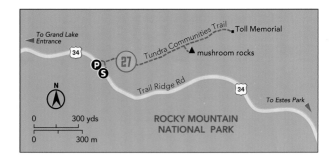

The first thing anyone will notice—even fit hikers who have spent a lot of time at altitude—is the decreased amount of oxygen at the Tundra Communities Trailhead. Unless you've ridden a bicycle up Trail Ridge Road to this point (which a handful of people do, but usually not to get to a hiking trail) or walked (which no one does), you'll step out of a car without much acclimation to the altitude. This is the highest trailhead in Rocky Mountain National Park, and the thin air and great views across the alpine tundra are good reasons to take your time and enjoy a stroll around. You may be lucky enough to see pika, marmots, or ptarmigans, the only year-round residents of the alpine tundra, or hear the pika or marmots communicating with each other.

The trail is paved with asphalt here for a reason—the alpine tundra is very fragile at this altitude, and the paved path protects the plant life as long as everyone stays on the trail. It can be tempting to step off the trail to take a photo, but don't. Just a few people stepping off the asphalt in one day can kill delicate plants.

The path climbs up 150 vertical feet in the first 0.3 mile (0.5 km), and then the grade eases. A side trail on the right (south) at 0.4 mile (0.6 km) leads up and into the schist "mushroom rock" monoliths for some interesting up-close views of the geology in this area. The main trail continues to its terminus at 0.5 mile (0.8 km) at another set of schist

Looking south from near the end of the Tundra Communities Trail

monoliths and the memorial plaque for former Rocky Mountain National Park superintendent Roger Toll, who was also superintendent of Mount Rainier and Yellowstone National Parks (and who is also the namesake of 12,979-foot [3956 m] Mount Toll, in the Indian Peaks Wilderness just south of Rocky Mountain National Park). A short, optional scramble up the rocks here leads to a circular brass map mounted on the rock, showing the distance to various national parks and mountains from this spot. From here, turn around the way you came to head back to the trailhead.

28 LAKE IRENE

Distance: 1 mile (1.6 km)
Elevation gain: 100 feet (31 m)
High point: 10,660 feet (3249 m)
Difficulty: Easy
Trail surface: Dirt and rock
Maps: USGS Fall River Pass, National Geographic Trails Illustrated Map 200: Rocky Mountain National Park
GPS: 40.413988°, –105.819069°
Notes: High altitude; be aware of exposure to afternoon thunderstorms; toilet at trailhead

Enjoy a short, easy walk to a quiet lake and a viewpoint tucked behind a picnic area just off Trail Ridge Road.

GETTING THERE

From the Estes Park Visitor Center, turn left (west) onto US Highway 34 (Big Thompson Avenue) and drive 0.2 mile (0.3 km), merging onto US 36 (Elkhorn Avenue) for 0.4 mile (0.6 km). Turn left to stay on US 36 and follow it west for 3.8 miles (6.1 km) into Rocky Mountain National Park, through the Beaver Meadows Entrance Station. After the entrance station,

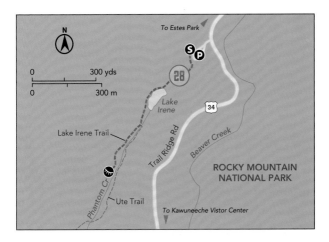

continue 2.9 miles (4.7 km) on US 36 to Deer Ridge Junction, and continue straight (the left fork), now on Trail Ridge Road. From the junction, drive another 21.9 miles (35.2 km), turning right (west) into the Lake Irene picnic area parking lot.

From the Kawuneeche Visitor Center, drive north on US 34 for 15.8 miles (25.4 km), turning left (west) into the Lake Irene picnic area parking lot.

ON THE TRAIL

Lake Irene isn't a much-talked-about destination in the park with swarms of people circling the parking lot waiting for their turn—it's a tucked-away, quiet walk, discovered by those driving Trail Ridge Road and stopping out of curiosity, or the folks here to make use of one of the eight picnic tables who then decided to go for a stroll around the peaceful tree-lined lake. The short walk is family-friendly and doable for small children, and the final 0.1 mile to the viewpoint is a great bonus if your young ones are capable. Deer can often be spotted in the area.

The main trail begins to the left (south) of a large log building and goes downhill via a set of log stairs. (A set of

The level trail along the west edge of Lake Irene is great for families.

stone steps at the southwest end of the parking loop also descends to join the main trail.) Follow the path as it descends gradually on log steps to reach the north end of Lake Irene after about 500 feet (152 m). The path continues along the lakeshore until 0.25 mile (0.4 km), where it continues past the end of the lake, still descending gradually. Just remember that you have to go back up this hill, which might feel steeper on the way back up to the trailhead. At 0.4 mile (0.6 km), you arrive at a junction; take the right (west) fork to reach a viewpoint of a meadow just below; on a clear day you can also see the peaks of the Gore Range, about 50 miles (80 km) to the southwest.

Turn around and return to the trail junction, and head back up the trail you came down (the west fork). A social trail traverses the slope on the opposite side of the lake and is another option for the return, but it isn't officially maintained and can be muddy at times.

29 DEER MOUNTAIN

Distance: **6.2 miles (10 km)**
Elevation gain: **1200 feet (366 m)**
High point: **10,013 feet (3052 m)**
Difficulty: **Medium**
Trail surface: **Dirt, rock**
Maps: **USGS Estes Park, National Geographic Trails Illustrated Map 200: Rocky Mountain National Park**
GPS: **40.386981°, –105.609883°**
Notes: **High altitude; be aware of exposure to afternoon thunderstorms**

> One of the lower-elevation summit hikes in the park, this route stays just below tree line but still offers rewarding views of the Continental Divide and Moraine Park.

GETTING THERE

From the Estes Park Visitor Center, turn left (west) onto US Highway 34 (Big Thompson Avenue) and drive 0.2 mile (0.3 km), merging onto US 36 (Elkhorn Avenue) for 0.4 mile (0.6 km). Turn left to stay on US 36 and follow it west for 3.8 miles into Rocky Mountain National Park, through the Beaver

Meadows Entrance Station. After the entrance station, continue 2.9 miles to Deer Ridge Junction. There are parallel parking spaces on both sides of the road here, and the trail begins on the north side of the road. Parking at the trailhead is limited, so an early-morning start is advised. Late afternoon can be a good time to get a parking spot for this hike too—just make sure you have enough time to get to the top and back before sunset.

HIDDEN VALLEY SKI AREA

From 1955 to 1991, Rocky Mountain National Park was home to the Hidden Valley Ski Area, on the east side of the park just off Trail Ridge Road, 2.4 miles (3.9 km) west of Deer Ridge Junction. The resort had twenty-seven runs, two T-bar lifts, two platter lifts, a double chairlift, a base lodge, and a parking lot for five hundred vehicles. The lifts and lodge were removed, but the ski runs can still be seen at Hidden Valley, which is now used as a sledding area in the winter.

ON THE TRAIL

The trail starts on the north side of the road, just left (west) of an information kiosk. After ascending a set of log steps, you come to a junction at 0.1 mile (160 m)—stay straight (right), following the sign to Deer Mountain Summit. The wide, sandy trail gradually climbs into a forest of ponderosa and other pines, and for most of the hike, you enjoy intermittent views of the surrounding mountains and the Moraine Park Valley down and to the south. At 0.2 mile (0.3 km), there is a viewpoint to the right (south) that's worth stopping at to take in the view of the mountains of the Continental Divide. If

OPPOSITE: *Just one of the many views on the Deer Mountain Trail*

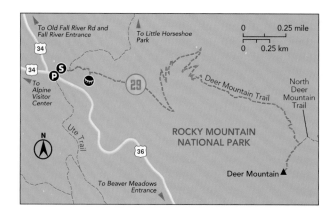

you're a wildflower connoisseur, look for mountain harebell, Bigelow's tansyaster, mountain gumweed, scarlet paint-brush, and others in this area. The trail continues to climb gradually, beginning to switchback up Deer Mountain's west slopes at the 0.8-mile mark (1.3 km). As the trail heads west, see if you can make out Trail Ridge Road cutting through the trees on the neighboring mountain directly to the west of Deer Mountain.

As you climb up the switchbacks for the next mile, take care to stay on the trail—you may notice evidence of other hikers cutting switchbacks, going straight up and down the hillsides—this is an amateur move, and destroys the trail and the surrounding environment by inducing erosion. And it doesn't save any time or energy. At about mile 2 (3.2 km), the switchbacks end as the trail flattens out and passes a couple of stands of aspens among the evergreen trees, and you traverse east and south across the flat top of Deer Mountain, with a few ups and downs.

At the trail junction at mile 2.9 (4.7 km), turn right (south-west), following the sign to the Deer Mountain Summit, and climb the last 180 vertical feet (55 m) to the summit via stone steps and trail. At the top, there are still some trees, but walk around a bit and you'll enjoy views to the south of Longs Peak (14,259 feet/4346 m), Chiefs Head Peak (13,579 feet/4139 m), Taylor Peak (13,153 feet/4009 m), and Hallett Peak (12,713 feet/3875 m), and to the north, Ypsilon Mountain (13,514 feet/4119 m), Hagues Peak (13,560 feet/4133 m), Mummy Mountain (13,425 feet/4092 m), and even Lumpy Ridge, Estes Park, and Estes Lake to the east. When you're done appreciating the view, return the way you came.

30 UTE TRAIL FROM FALL RIVER PASS TO MILNER PASS

Distance: **4.1 miles (6.9 km)—one-way**
Elevation gain: **150 feet elevation gain (46 m), 1000 feet elevation loss (305 m)**
High point: **11,764 feet (3586 m)**
Difficulty: **Medium**
Trail surface: **Dirt, rock**
Maps: **USGS Fall River Pass, National Geographic Trails Illustrated Map 200: Rocky Mountain National Park**
GPS: **40.440944°, –105.755747°**
Notes: **Shuttle hike (two cars needed); high altitude; be aware of exposure to afternoon thunderstorms; toilet at trailhead**

This primarily downhill one-way hike from the Alpine Visitor Center to Milner Pass delivers big views across high-alpine tundra.

GETTING THERE
From the Estes Park Visitor Center, turn left (west) onto US Highway 34 (Big Thompson Avenue) and drive 0.2 mile (0.3 km), merging onto US 36 (Elkhorn Avenue) for 0.4 mile (0.6 km). Turn left to stay on US 36 and follow it west for 3.8

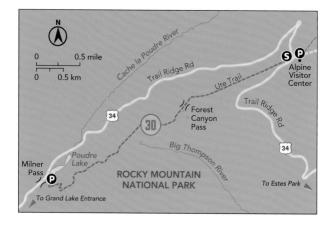

miles (6.1 km) into Rocky Mountain National Park, through the Beaver Meadows Entrance Station. After the entrance station, continue 2.9 miles (4.7 km) to Deer Ridge Junction, and continue straight (the left fork) at the junction. From the junction, drive another 17 miles (27.4 km), turning right (north) into the Alpine Visitor Center parking lot.

ON THE TRAIL

One of the unsung benefits of a curvy, high-altitude thoroughfare like Trail Ridge Road is that it enables hikes like this one: one of the more low-effort ways to experience a lot of alpine tundra with very little uphill travel. Since it involves a shuttle, you'll need to park a car at either end, or, if you've got a friend who's willing to forego hiking and drop you off at the start and pick you up at the finish, that works too. This can be a nice option if you want to hike, but your traveling companion wants to have a more relaxing day checking out the Alpine Visitor Center and/or having a coffee and snacks while you're on the trail.

OPPOSITE: *Meadows of wildflowers can be found along the Ute Trail.*

The Ute Trail begins across Trail Ridge Road on the west side of the road at the end of a marked crosswalk. In the first mile, looking straight ahead over the trail, you can see the Never Summer Mountains, the 10-mile-long (16-km-long) range that runs north to south along the park's western border and is home to several 12,000-foot-plus (3658 m) peaks. Look down to see wildflowers: alpine avens, elephant head, moss campion, and others, among other tundra shrubs and bushes. At about 0.5 mile (0.8 km), the trail climbs about 50 feet (15 m)—sorry, it's not all downhill—before resuming the descent. At mile 1.5 (1.6 km), pass by a tarn on the left (east), with views of Mount Julian (12,928 feet/3940 m) in the distance behind it. At 1.7 miles (2.7 km), cross Forest Canyon Pass, elevation 11,520 feet (3511 m), and continue dropping while subalpine fir trees begin to appear as you gradually pass through tree line. The forest begins to thicken around the trail, and at mile 2.5 (4 km) you enter another nice section of wildflowers: scarlet paintbrush, elephant head, and others. Shortly after that, cross a series of small streams that flow over the trail, and at around 3.1 miles (5 km), the trees tighten as the trail winds through them, beginning to drop the final 400 feet (122 m) to Milner Pass. At the trail junction at 3.4 miles (5.5 km), take the sharp right (north) fork, following a sign to Milner Pass, and head downhill on a set of stone steps. After this point, the trail begins to drop more steeply via log steps and switchbacks.

At 4.1 miles (6.6 km), you see Poudre Lake. The trail will trace its southern shore on its way to the parking lot, where your ride (hopefully) awaits.

GOING FARTHER

If you'd prefer to get an uphill workout, go ahead and do this hike in reverse, starting at Milner Pass and ending at the Alpine Visitor Center.

31 UPPER BEAVER MEADOWS LOOP

Distance: 5 miles (8 km)
Elevation gain: 935 feet (285 m)
High point: 9235 feet (2815 m)
Difficulty: Medium
Trail surface: Dirt, rock
Maps: USGS McHenrys Peak, USGS Longs Peak, USGS Trail Ridge, USGS Estes Park, National Geographic Trails Illustrated Map 200: Rocky Mountain National Park
GPS: 40.372919°, –105.614044°
Notes: High altitude; be aware of exposure to afternoon thunderstorms; toilet at trailhead

This underrated (and thus, undercrowded) short loop hike travels through both dense forests and open meadows, which provide views of the peaks of the Continental Divide.

GETTING THERE

From the Estes Park Visitor Center, turn left (west) onto US Highway 34 (Big Thompson Avenue) and drive 0.2 mile (0.3 km), merging onto US 36 (Elkhorn Avenue) for 0.4 mile (0.6 km). Turn left to stay on US 36 and follow it west for 3.8 miles (6.1 km) into Rocky Mountain National Park, through the Beaver Meadows Entrance Station. After the entrance station, continue 0.8 mile (1.3 km), turning left (northwest) onto Upper Beaver Meadows Road, just after a sharp right-hand curve. Drive 1.5 miles (2.4 km) on Upper Beaver Meadows Road to the trailhead at the end of the road.

ON THE TRAIL

From the parking lot, walk about 400 feet (122 m) east on the dirt road you drove in on and, at a sign for Beaver Mountain Trail, turn left onto a trail that angles northeast off the road.

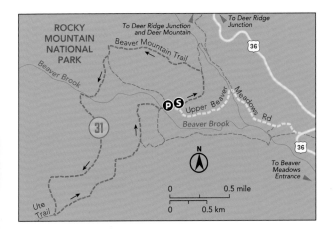

In this first section, a variety of wildflowers can be seen: yarrow, foothills arnica, asters, and others. As the trail climbs slightly during the first 0.3 mile (0.5 km), take a moment to look south at the view of the Continental Divide. At 0.4 mile (0.6 km), the trail turns west and drops slightly into the next valley, reaching a junction a few hundred feet farther. Take the left (northwest) fork, following the sign for the Beaver Mountain Trail, and start climbing gradually through ponderosa pines and aspens.

At 1.3 miles (2.1 km), the trail begins to drop downhill, and at 1.6 miles (2.6 km), reaches a junction with an unmarked trail—continue right (south) and cross a log bridge over a stream. At 2 miles (3.2 km), the trail crosses Beaver Brook and begins climbing through a thick forest of lodgepole pines. In the next half mile (0.8 km), in stark contrast to the earlier part of this hike, the trees are so thick that you can scarcely make out the silhouette of Deer Mountain (10,013 feet/3052 m), about 1.5 miles (2.4 km) directly east through the trees. At mile 2.5 (4 km), the trees open up again to reveal views of Deer Mountain, Twin Sisters Peaks (11,428 feet/3483 m),

OPPOSITE: *A stand of ponderosa pines on the Upper Beaver Meadows Loop*

Longs Peak (14,259 feet/4346 m), Pagoda Mountain (13,497 feet/4114 m), and Chiefs Head Peak (13,579 feet/4139 m). A few hundred feet later, take in the view of the Moraine Park valley below and to your left (southeast), and the Big Thompson River meandering its way through the middle of the Moraine Park.

At 2.9 miles (4.7 km) are a hitch rack and a confusing junction of social trails—your trail continues uphill to the right (west). The trail pops around the corner to a view of Notchtop Mountain (12,129 feet/3697 m) to the southeast and the Ptarmigan Glacier to the left (east) of Notchtop. At the 3.2-mile mark (5.2 km), the trail starts to drop in elevation through the forest and reaches a trail junction with the Ute Trail at mile 3.5 (5.6 km). Go left (northeast), following the sign for the closer of the two Beaver Mountain Trailheads listed on the sign. The route now joins the Ute Trail and descends a steep 500 feet (152 m) in the next mile. At 4.6 miles (7.4 km), you hit your last trail junction—stay left, following the sign to the Beaver Meadows Trailhead.

GOING FARTHER

The Upper Beaver Meadows Loop intersects a handful of trails, and many variations are possible, including hiking Tombstone Ridge via the Ute Trail (Hike 32) and joining this loop at the 3.5-mile mark (5.6 km), provided you have someone to drop you off at the Ute Trail and pick you up at the Upper Beaver Meadows Trailhead, or hiking Deer Mountain (Hike 29) from this trailhead.

32 TOMBSTONE RIDGE VIA UTE TRAIL

Distance: 3.4 miles (5.5 km)
Elevation gain: 1000 feet (305 m)
High point: 11,655 feet (3552 m)

Difficulty: Medium

Trail surface: Dirt, rock

Maps: USGS Trail Ridge, National Geographic Trails Illustrated Map 200: Rocky Mountain National Park

GPS: 40.393361°, −105.695383°

Notes: High altitude; be aware of exposure to afternoon thunderstorms; limited parking

> This short, wide-open, and uncrowded sampler of high-alpine terrain and views gets you just far enough away from the traffic of Trail Ridge Road for a bit of solitude.

GETTING THERE

From the Estes Park Visitor Center, turn left (west) onto US Highway 34 (Big Thompson Avenue) and drive 0.2 mile (0.3 km), merging onto US 36 (Elkhorn Avenue) for 0.4 mile (0.6 km). Turn left to stay on US 36 and follow it west for 3.8 miles (6.1 km) into Rocky Mountain National Park, through the Beaver Meadows Entrance Station. After the entrance

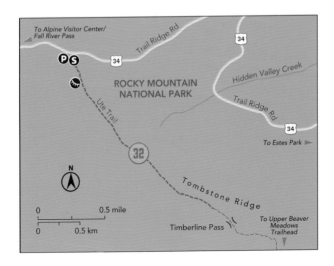

station, continue 2.9 miles (4.7 km) to Deer Ridge Junction, and continue straight (take the left fork) at the junction. From the junction, drive another 10 miles (16.1 km), watching for the unsigned Ute Trailhead on the left (south) and a handful of parallel parking spots on the side of Trail Ridge Road. An early start is advised because of the limited amount of parking at the trailhead, as well as the complete lack of cover in case of afternoon thunderstorms.

ON THE TRAIL

The main thing to consider with this hike, as you're ambling along and enjoying the high-altitude views, is when to decide to turn around. There's no lake or summit, or even a sign at the turnaround point of this out-and-back hike, but the trail does begin to drop off more steeply about 1.5 miles (2.4 km) from the trailhead—so unless you really want a workout hiking back uphill, the ideal place to turn around is at about 1.7 miles (2.7 km).

From the parking area, the Ute Trail heads south on a very rocky dirt trail. The rocks, in addition to the fact that you're hiking at 11,400 feet (3475 m), can make it feel difficult to get any momentum going, which is fine—it's a short hike, so take your time and enjoy the views. Remember to stay on the trail at all times to keep the fragile alpine tundra intact—just a few footfalls a day can kill the plants at this altitude. At 0.1 mile (160 m), a short side trail to the right (southwest) leads to a viewpoint of Mount Julian (12,928 feet/3940 m), which is worth a stop before continuing down the main trail. At 0.2 mile (0.3 km), the trail rounds a corner to views to the south of Longs Peak (14,259 feet/4346 m), Pagoda Mountain (13,497 feet/4114 m), and Hallett Peak (12,713 feet/3875 m). Up closer to the trail, keep your eyes out for marmots roving around the adjacent boulder field (you may also hear

OPPOSITE: *The Ute Trail heads across open tundra, looking toward Longs Peak in the distance.*

them chatting with each other as you approach, if they're out there). After a brief initial climb over the first 0.3 mile (0.5 km), the trail flattens out for the next 0.75 mile (1.2 km). Enjoy the walking and the views here—the trail is headed for Timberline Pass, at 11,484 feet (3500 m), at about 2 miles (3.2 km) from the trailhead. Tree line is actually a few hundred feet on the other side of Timberline Pass, at about 11,240 feet (3426 m).

At 1.4 miles (2.3 km), Twin Sisters Peaks (11,428 feet/3483 m) and Estes Cone (11,006 feet/3355 m) come into view, and at 1.5 miles (2.4 km), the trail starts to trend downhill. If you continue farther, just keep in mind you have to walk back uphill to your car—a small rock tower on the left (north) side of the trail at about 1.7 miles (2.7 km) marks where the terrain starts dropping more steeply, and beyond that the trail

Wildflowers along the Ute Trail

becomes less defined and follows cairns. Turn around here for a 3.4-mile (5.5 km) out-and-back. Or continue on to just before the 2-mile mark (3.2 km), where the view below opens up a little bit and you can make out the green Moraine Park Valley to the southeast, and even Lake Estes and part of the town of Estes Park to the east. To return to the trailhead, retrace your steps back up the trail.

GOING FARTHER

With a shuttle, either by parking a car at each end, or recruiting a friend to drop you off at the Ute Trailhead and pick you up at the Upper Beaver Meadows Trailhead at the end of your hike, you could walk the Ute Trail all the way down to the Upper Beaver Meadows Trailhead, an almost all-downhill hike totaling about 6.3 miles (10.1 km).

GRAND LAKE ENTRANCE

The west side of Rocky Mountain National Park is much quieter than the east side: Only 17 percent of the traffic entering the park comes through the Grand Lake Entrance on the west, as opposed to the other entrances, all on the east side. The west side doesn't deliver the big views of the Continental Divide right out your vehicle window, but it is beautiful in its own right and has a rich history from early American Indian exploration, attempts at mining, and tourism beginning in the early twentieth century after the completion of Trail Ridge Road linked it to the east side of the park.

As you enter the park via the Grand Lake Entrance, the Colorado River runs parallel to US Highway 34 to the west. It is a calm, narrow stream here in the Kawuneeche Valley, compared to the giant it becomes as it makes its way toward the Gulf of California hundreds of miles southwest. High peaks parallel the river on both sides: the Never Summer Mountains rising to the west outside the park boundary, and the Front Range to the east, as well as all the mountains inside Rocky Mountain National Park. Trails and trailheads on this side of the park are more spread out but are still popular during the busy season. There is only one national park campground on the west side, the Timber Creek Campground (see Contacts).

OPPOSITE: *The Colorado River is pretty tame on the trail to the Holzwarth Historic Site (Hike 34).*

33 COYOTE VALLEY

Distance: 1 mile (1.6 km)
Elevation gain: 15 feet (5 m)
High point: 8830 feet (2691 m)
Difficulty: Easy
Trail surface: Crushed rock
Maps: USGS Grand Lake, National Geographic Trails Illustrated
Map 200: Rocky Mountain National Park
GPS: 40.344597°, −105.858320°
Notes: High altitude; be aware of exposure to afternoon
thunderstorms; toilet at trailhead; catch-and-keep fishing

A flat, ADA-accessible path winds along the Colorado River
and the Kawuneeche Valley, offering the possibility of seeing
elk, moose, beaver, muskrats, coyotes, and other wildlife.

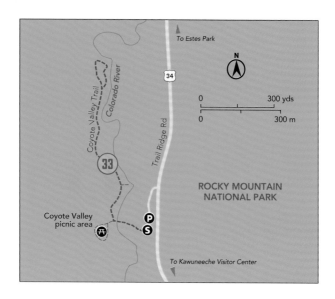

GETTING THERE

From the Estes Park Visitor Center, turn left (west) onto US Highway 34 (Big Thompson Avenue) and drive 0.2 mile (0.3 km), merging onto US 36 (Elkhorn Avenue) for 0.4 mile (0.6 km). Turn left to stay on US 36 and follow it west for 3.8 miles (6.1 km) into Rocky Mountain National Park, through the Beaver Meadows Entrance Station. After the entrance station, continue 2.9 miles (4.7 km) to Deer Ridge Junction, and continue straight (take the left fork) at the junction. From the junction, drive another 31.8 miles (51.2 km) on Trail Ridge Road, turning right (west) into the Coyote Valley Trail parking lot.

From the Kawuneeche Visitor Center, drive north on US 34 for 5.9 miles (9.5 km), turning left (west) into the Coyote Valley Trail parking lot.

ON THE TRAIL

The Coyote Valley Trail is unique in Rocky Mountain National Park, a place known more for the up-close views of its rocky peaks and high altitude—here, you'll walk along the bottom of a wide valley hewn by glaciers, beside a calm, narrow, shallow section of the Colorado River. The glacier that once occupied the Kawuneeche Valley was 1500 feet (457 m) thick at this point. As you walk along this path, imagine 150 stories of ice piled above your head. Parts of that glacier still remain in the Never Summer Mountains, rising above the valley to the west.

Overall, the trail is flat and wide and has plenty of benches for rest stops, but those using wheelchairs or strollers should know that the first 200 feet (61 m) of the trail leaving the parking lot are as steep as 10 percent in grade; it's downhill on the way out and uphill on the way back.

Just after the initial downslope of the trail, cross the Colorado River via a stone bridge and pass the Coyote Valley

A view of the Kawuneeche Valley from the Coyote Valley Trail

picnic area on the south side of the trail, as the trail turns north to parallel the river and the valley. At this point, the Colorado River is a small stream compared to the mighty river it becomes as it gathers snowmelt and water from tributaries in the 1400-plus miles (2253 km) it travels from here almost all the way to the Gulf of California.

Several interpretive signs along the path detail the natural and human history of the Kawuneeche Valley, including American Indian use (the Arapaho word *kawuneeche* translates to "coyote valley"), homesteading, and dude ranches. One remnant of the mining efforts in the area, the Grand Ditch, can be seen tracing a straight line across the southeast flank of 12,397-foot (3779 m) Baker Mountain across the valley. Built in the late 1800s to divert water from the mountains down to the valley, the Grand Ditch is now a hiking trail.

The trail parallels the river, passing a few fishing spots (primarily brook trout), and ends at a short lollipop loop at 0.5 mile (0.8 km). From the loop, head back the way you came to return to the trailhead.

34 HOLZWARTH HISTORIC SITE

Distance: 1.3 miles (2.1 km)
Elevation gain: 75 feet (23 m)
High point: 8935 feet (2723 m)
Difficulty: Easy
Trail surface: Packed gravel
Maps: USGS Grand Lake, National Geographic Trails Illustrated Map 200: Rocky Mountain National Park
GPS: 40.372851°, –105.854469°
Notes: High altitude; be aware of exposure to afternoon thunderstorms; toilet at trailhead; catch-and-keep fishing

This casual hike visits the historic buildings of the Holzwarth Trout Lodge, a rustic resort built in the early 1900s.

GETTING THERE
From the Estes Park Visitor Center, turn left (west) onto US Highway 34 (Big Thompson Avenue) and drive 0.2 mile (0.3 km), merging onto US 36 (Elkhorn Avenue) for 0.4 mile (0.6 km). Turn left to stay on US 36 and follow it west for 3.8 miles (6.1 km) into Rocky Mountain National Park, through the Beaver Meadows Entrance Station. After the entrance station, continue 2.9 miles (4.7 km) to Deer Ridge Junction, and continue straight (take the left fork) at the junction. From the junction, drive another 29.9 miles (48.1 km) on Trail

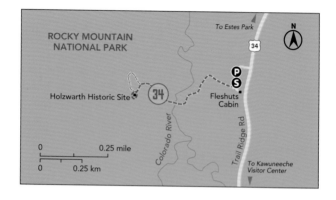

Ridge Road, turning right (west) into the Holzwarth Historic Site parking lot.

From the Kawuneeche Visitor Center, drive 7.9 miles (12.7 km) north on US Highway 34, and turn left (west) into the Holzwarth Historic Site parking lot.

ON THE TRAIL

From the south end of the parking lot, a short trail leads to the Fleshuts Cabin, built by Joseph Fleshuts in 1902, when the Colorado River flowed right in front of the cabin (it later altered its course, moving about 500 feet/152 m to the west). Fleshuts attempted to make a living selling goods to miners in the area, but the miners didn't have much luck, so his business didn't either, and he left in 1911. American Indian tribes, the Ute and Arapaho, had been coming to the valley to hunt since at least the early 1800s—but they didn't construct any buildings.

The trail continues west, crossing the Colorado River on a bridge at about 0.3 mile (0.5 km) and continuing to the Holzwarth site. John and Sophia Holzwarth were German immigrants who operated a saloon in Denver until it was closed by state Prohibition laws in 1916. In 1917, they came to the Kawuneeche Valley to build a ranch. Their second summer

Historic equipment along the trail to the Holzwarth Historic Site

here, John was injured in a wagon accident, leaving him unable to handle ranch work. Fortunately, in 1920, Fall River Road was completed, opening a second avenue for tourists wanting to reach to this side of the Continental Divide, and the Holzwarths reimagined their ranch as the Holzwarth Trout Lodge.

At about 0.5 mile (0.8 km), you'll reach the grounds of the old trout lodge and can explore the area. The Mama Cabin was the first cabin built here, and the majority of the other outbuildings were built between 1920 and 1945.

The business flourished for almost a decade, and in 1929 the Holzwarths began building the nearby Never Summer Ranch, and the trout lodge buildings served primarily as overflow lodging for Never Summer Ranch guests. John and Sophia had four children, and their son Johnnie continued to operate the guest ranch until 1973, when he donated the property to The Nature Conservancy. In 1974, The Nature Conservancy turned the property over to the National Park Service and it became part of Rocky Mountain National Park, after which the buildings of the Never Summer Ranch were removed.

When you're finished exploring the historic buildings, retrace your steps and return to the trailhead the way you came.

35 BIG MEADOWS FROM GREEN MOUNTAIN TRAILHEAD

Distance: **4.8 miles (7.7 km)**
Elevation gain: **800 feet (244 m)**
High point: **9475 feet (2888 m)**
Difficulty: **Medium**
Trail surface: **Dirt, rock**
Maps: **USGS Grand Lake, National Geographic Trails Illustrated Map 200: Rocky Mountain National Park**
GPS: **40.307406°, –105.841216°**
Notes: **High altitude; be aware of exposure to afternoon thunderstorms; toilet at trailhead**

> On the park's lesser-visited west side, this hike visits an alpine meadow and offers mountain views and the possibility of seeing moose and elk.

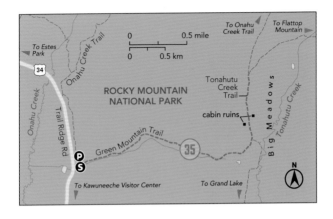

GETTING THERE

From the Estes Park Visitor Center, turn left (west) onto US Highway 34 (Big Thompson Avenue) and drive 0.2 mile (0.3 km), merging onto US 36 (Elkhorn Avenue) for 0.4 mile (0.6 km). Turn left to stay on US 36 and follow it west for 3.8 miles (6.1 km) into Rocky Mountain National Park, through the Beaver Meadows Entrance Station. After the entrance station, continue 2.9 miles (4.7 km) to Deer Ridge Junction, and continue straight (take the left fork) at the junction. From the junction, drive another 34.8 miles (56 km) on Trail Ridge Road, turning left (east) into the Green Mountain Trailhead parking lot.

From the Kawuneeche Visitor Center, drive north on US 34 for 2.9 miles (4.7 km), turning right (east) into the Green Mountain Trailhead parking lot.

ON THE TRAIL

The trail leaves from the southeast corner of the parking lot and immediately climbs next to a creek. Keep your eyes open for elk and moose during this hike. If you encounter any near or on the trail, be careful to give them a wide berth (and the right-of-way). The wildflowers begin almost immediately as well: heartleaf arnica, mountain harebell, yarrow, Bigelow's tansyaster, and others. At about the half-mile point (0.8 km), the trail flattens out for about a half mile (0.8 km), then resumes climbing, but more gradually. This hike follows a section of trail also utilized by the Continental Divide National Scenic Trail (also known as the CDT), a 3100-mile (4989 km) National Scenic Trail from Canada to Mexico along the Continental Divide—so if you do this entire hike, you can say you've hiked about seven-hundredths of 1 percent of the CDT.

At 1.6 miles (2.6 km), a couple of social trails head off to the right (south)—stay left on the main trail. At 1.7 miles (2.7 km), reach a junction with the trail to the Green Mountain backcountry campsite; again, stay left (east) to continue to Big Meadows. From here, the trail drops downhill for another 0.1 mile (160 m) to the first view of Big Meadows and the junction with the Tonahutu Creek Trail. Many people choose to end the hike here, but continuing on another half mile along the west edge of the meadow brings a few different views and a chance to see some historic cabin ruins so keep going. Take the Tonahutu Creek Trail to the left (north), following the sign to Upper Tonahutu. As you walk along the west side of Big Meadows, you'll come upon two sets of ruins left by Sam Stone, who tried to produce hay here in the meadow around the turn of the twentieth century—the Green Mountain Trail, the first 1.8 miles (2.9 km) of trail you hiked, was a wagon road for him.

Around the meadow, you have views of Mount Ida (12,880 feet/3926 m), Nakai Peak (12,216 feet/3723 m), and Mount Patterson (11,424 feet/3482 m), and if you're lucky, you may spot moose or elk around the meadow. The best chance of seeing moose and elk is first thing in the morning or around dusk. At 2.4 miles (3.9 km), reach another trail junction—turn around here and retrace your steps to return to the trailhead.

GOING FARTHER

If you continue north at the junction at 2.4 miles (3.9 km), you can create a loop hike back to the Green Mountain Trailhead using the Onahu Creek Trail. This option adds 5.1 miles (8.2 km) and about 500 feet (152 m) of elevation gain, for a total of 7.5 miles (12.1 km).

OPPOSITE: *Historic cabin ruins at the western edge of Big Meadows*

CONTACTS

**Rocky Mountain
National Park**
www.nps.gov/romo

Campgrounds:
www.nps.gov/romo
/planyourvisit/camping.htm

Fishing Regulations:
www.nps.gov/romo
/planyourvisit/fishing.htm

Alpine Visitor Center
Open: 9:00 AM–5:00 PM
Memorial Day weekend
through Columbus Day,
depending on weather
Location: Fall River Pass at
the junction of Trail Ridge
and Old Fall River Roads
Phone: (970) 586-1206

**Beaver Meadows
Visitor Center**
Open: 9:00 AM–4:30 PM year-
round, closed holidays
Location: 1000 US 36,
Estes Park, CO 80517
Phone: (970) 586-1206

Fall River Visitor Center
Open: Hours vary by season
Location: 3450 Fall River
Road, Estes Park, CO 80517
Phone: (970) 586-1206

Kawuneeche Visitor Center
Open: Hours vary by season
Location: 16018 US 34,
Grand Lake, CO 80447
Phone: (970) 627-3471

OPPOSITE: *The Colorado River along the Coyote Valley Trail (Hike 33)*

Estes Park

Estes Park Mountain Shop
(gear and apparel,
equipment rentals,
guided trips)
Location: 2050 Big
Thompson Avenue,
Estes Park, CO 80517
Phone: (970) 586-6548
www.estesparkmountain
shop.com

Estes Park Visitor Center

Location: 500 Big Thompson
Avenue, Estes Park,
CO 80517
Phone: (970) 577-9900
www.visitestespark.com

Wildflowers along the Moraine Park Loop (Hike 11)

INDEX

Alberta Falls 36, 59–62, 68, 101
Alpine Ridge Trail 164–166
alpine tundra plants 21
Alpine Visitor Center 23, 30
altitude sickness 42
Arrowhead 104
Aspenglen Campground 33

backcountry camping 37–38
Batman Rock 120
Bear Lake 25, 36, 56–58, 75, 107
Bear Lake Interpretive hike 25
Bear Lake Trail 25, 56–58
Bear Lake Road 33, 55–108
bears 19
Beaver Meadows Visitor Center 30
Bierstadt Lake 90–94, 107
Bierstadt Lake Loop 90–94
Big Meadows from Green Mountain
    Trailhead 198–201
Big Thompson River 61, 68, 84, 89,
    97, 98, 184
bighorn sheep 13, 19, 23–24
Black Canyon Trail 119–125
Black Lake hike, 99–104
Book, The 121
Bookmark Pinnacle 121
Bridal Veil Falls from Cow Creek
    Trailhead 115–119

Calypso Cascades 139
campfires 38, 39, 40
Chasm Lake hike 151–155
Chiefs Head Peak 62, 68, 70, 101,
    103, 104, 176, 184
Colorado Highway 7 127–161
Continental Divide 13, 25, 55, 64, 65,
    84, 93, 94, 114, 124, 176, 181, 183
Continental Divide National Scenic
    Trail 200
Copeland Falls 133–136, 139, 140
Copeland Falls hike 133–136
Cow Creek 118, 123, 124

Coyote Valley hike 192–195
Cub Lake 27, 84, 86, 90
Cub Lake hike 82–86
Deer Mountain 28, 176, 183
Deer Mountain hike 173–177
Devils Gulch Road 111–125
difficulty 50
distance 49
dogs 36, 141
Dream Lake 81, 107
drones 38

elevation gain 47
elk 13, 14, 17, 19, 55, 84, 97, 98,
    199, 201
Estes Cone 129, 132, 144–147,
    149, 188
Estes Cone via Longs Peak hike
    144–147
Estes Park 13, 23, 25, 30, 31,
    107114, 124, 143, 177, 189
Estes Park Visitor Center 27, 30, 49,
    51, 55
Eugenia Mine 146

Fall River Pass 23, 25, 30
Fall River Visitor Center 30
fees 35, 36
Fern Falls 90
Fern Lake 90
Fern Lake hike 86–90
firearms 38
fish 20, 36, 73–74, 103, 129, 139,
    195
fishing 36, 49, 65, 73, 81, 90, 129,
    195
Flattop Mountain 55, 77, 81, 94, 108
Flattop Mountain hike 104–109
Forest Canyon Overlook 24–25
Four Lakes Loop hike 78–82

Gem Lake 115, 124
Gem Lake hike 112–115

Glacier Basin Campground 33–34
Glacier Gorge 62, 68, 70, 77, 101, 103, 107
Grand Lake 23, 25
Grand Lake Entrance 191–201

Hallett Peak 58, 81, 93, 108, 114, 124, 143, 177, 187
Hallett Peak hike 104–109
Hidden Valley Ski Area 176
Hiker Shuttle Express. 27, 30
Hikes at a Glance 9–11
history, human 13, 14–17, 23, 25, 36, 65, 84, 97, 118, 146–147, 174, 194–195, 196–198
Holzwarth Historic Site hike 195–198

Kawuneeche Valley 191, 193, 196–197
Kawuneeche Visitor Center 30
krummholz 21

Lake Haiyaha 81
Lake Irene 172
Lake Irene hike 170–173
Leave No Trace 39–42
Lily Lake 128, 129, 147
Lily Lake hike 128–130
Lily Mountain hike 140–143
Lily Ridge Trail 131–133
Loch, The 73, 74
Loch hike, The 71–74
Longs Peak 21, 24, 58, 62, 65, 68, 70, 77, 81, 94, 101, 103, 104, 107, 109, 114, 124, 127, 128, 132, 143, 144, 147, 149, 152, 153, 155–161
Longs Peak Campground 32, 34
Longs Peak via Keyhole Route 155–161
Lumpy Ridge 17, 30, 111, 112, 121, 123, 143, 177
Lumpy Ridge Loop 119–125

maps 50–51
marmots 13, 19–20, 55, 163, 168, 187–188
McHenrys Peak 62, 68, 101, 104, 114, 124
Mills Lake 70, 103
Mills Lake hike 66–70
Milner Pass 180
Moraine Park 36, 55, 84, 97, 176, 184, 189
Moraine Park Campground 32, 34
Moraine Park Loop 94–98
Mount Lady Washington 154, 158
Mount Meeker 114, 124, 127, 128, 132, 143, 144, 147, 149

Never Summer Mountains 17, 166, 178, 191, 193
North St. Vrain Creek 134, 139
Nymph Lake 80

Odessa Lake 77–78
Odessa Lake via Bear Lake Trailhead 74–78
Old Fall River Road 25
Ouzel Falls 137, 139

Pagoda Mountain 58, 62, 68, 70, 101, 103, 104, 183, 187
Park & Ride 27, 30, 55
Paul Bunyan's Boot 114, 124
permits 37
Powell Peak 114, 124

Rams Horn Mountain 143

safety 42–47
Sheep Lakes 19, 23–24
Spearhead 70, 103, 104
Sprague Lake 28, 36, 64, 65
Sprague Lake hike 62–65
Storm Peak 158

Taylor Peak 176
Three Waterfalls hike 136–140
thunderstorms 42–43
Timber Creek Campground 34, 191
Tombstone Ridge via Ute Trail 184–189
Trail Ridge Road 13, 16, 23, 25, 32, 108, 143, 163–189, 191
trees 20–21
Tundra Communities Trail 25, 163, 167–170
Twin Owls 111, 120
Twin Sisters Peaks 114, 124, 127, 131, 143, 147, 148–151, 183, 188
Twin Sisters Peaks hike 148–151

Upper Beaver Meadows Loop 181–184
Ute Trail from Fall River Pass to Milner Pass 177–180

weather 31, 42–43
wildflowers 20, 65, 77, 84, 89, 93, 118, 121, 123, 129, 147, 166, 180, 181, 200
wildfires 44, 84–85, 89
wildlife 13–14, 17, 19–20, 23–24, 38, 41, 55, 84, 97, 98, 163, 168, 187–188, 199, 201

Ypsilon Mountain 143, 150, 166, 177

recreation • lifestyle • conservation

MOUNTAINEERS BOOKS, including its two imprints, Skipstone and Braided River, is a leading publisher of quality outdoor recreation, sustainability, and conservation titles. As a 501(c)(3) nonprofit, we are committed to supporting the environmental and educational goals of our organization by providing expert information on human-powered adventure, sustainable practices at home and on the trail, and preservation of wilderness.

Our publications are made possible through the generosity of donors, and through sales of 700 titles on outdoor recreation, sustainable lifestyle, and conservation. To donate, purchase books, or learn more, visit us online:

MOUNTAINEERS BOOKS
1001 SW Klickitat Way, Suite 201 • Seattle, WA 98134 • 800-553-4453
mbooks@mountaineersbooks.org • www.mountaineersbooks.org

An independent nonprofit publisher since 1960

Mountaineers Books is proud to support the Leave No Trace Center for Outdoor Ethics, whose mission is to promote and inspire responsible outdoor recreation through education, research, and partnerships. The Leave No Trace program is focused specifically on human-powered (nonmotorized) recreation. For more information, visit www.lnt.org.

YOU MAY ALSO LIKE

ABOUT THE AUTHOR

Brendan Leonard's parents took him to visit Rocky Mountain National Park when he was seven years old, driving out from their native Iowa in a Buick Skyhawk coupe. It must have made an impression, as he relocated to Denver when he was twenty-six and stayed for more than a decade and a half. Rocky Mountain National Park became one of his regular haunts on the Front Range for hiking and trail

Photo by Hilary Oliver

running, rock climbing on Lumpy Ridge and some of the park's high peaks, and backcountry skiing. He has bicycled across America, run dozens of ultramarathons and marathons, and spent more than two months beneath the rim of the Grand Canyon.

Brendan is a columnist for *Outside* magazine and has written for dozens of outdoor and adventure publications, including *Adventure Journal*, *Alpinist*, *Climbing*, *Backpacker*, *Sierra*, and others. He has authored ten books, including a collection of humorous essays titled *Bears Don't Care About Your Problems*, and a climbing memoir, *Sixty Meters to Anywhere*. More of his work can be found at Semi-Rad.com.